Newman Smyth

The orthodox Theolgy of today

Newman Smyth

The orthodox Theolgy of today

ISBN/EAN: 9783743344990

Manufactured in Europe, USA, Canada, Australia, Japa

Cover: Foto ©Lupo / pixelio.de

Manufactured and distributed by brebook publishing software (www.brebook.com)

Newman Smyth

The orthodox Theolgy of today

THE

ORTHODOX THEOLOGY OF TO-DAY

BY

NEWMAN SMYTH

AUTHOR OF "THE RELIGIOUS FEELING" AND "OLD FAITHS IN NEW LIGHT"

NEW YORK

CHARLES SCRIBNER'S SONS

743 AND 745 BROADWAY

1881

TROW'S
PRINTING AND BOOKBINDING COMPANY
201–213 *East 12th Street*
NEW YORK

CONTENTS.

PREFACE.

THESE discourses were originally prepared in answer to certain objections which had been urged against evangelical teaching in the columns of a local newspaper in my own home, and which are often raised, in various forms, as difficulties in the way of the popular acceptance of the doctrines of the churches. They are now printed substantially as they were first delivered, as, in consenting to their publication, I have felt that the attempt to meet an expressed want in any one locality might prove the most hopeful fidelity to a real need of the larger public to which these discussions of some vital questions of Christian thought are now addressed.

Though they were in form a reply to misconceptions and objections urged upon the attention of the pulpit in behalf of popular scepticism, I trust that their spirit may not be found to be controversial. I have sought rather to avail myself of admitted difficulties and common perplexities concerning the doctrines of the churches, as a background upon which I would bring out the hopeful convictions and assured beliefs of those evangelical scholars with whom I find myself to be most in sympathy, and who, as it seems to me, are giving the simplest form, and the truest expression, to Christian theology at the present time. The positions and views of these Christian thinkers of to-day can hardly be measured or defined by any traditional lines of division, or by theological names derived from the past. The more recent phrases of ecclesiastical separation, "Old School" and "New School," represent to them issues of yesterday rather than of to-day; and the definitions and phraseology which some who still stand marking time in those old ways are careful to maintain, seem to them utterly inadequate determinations of the advanced line of Christian reasoning and belief which they are compelled to occupy, as they seek to face the great ques-

tions with which faith is now confronted. They
do not stoop down and watch anxiously lest
the "foundations" be shaken; but, knowing
that God's words cannot pass away, they are
eager to look up and face present responsibilities of Christian thought, and to catch what
revelations of truth may be dawning upon the
horizons of to-day.

While, thus, in common with an increasing
number of Christian thinkers I must disclaim the
terms, and decline myself to be classified by the
nomenclature of the schools, I would still retain
and use as descriptive of a reverent, but progressive, Christian theology the old word orthodoxy, especially since a distinction of no little
present importance is coming to be made, and
needs to be emphasized, between orthodoxy and
orthodoxism. By orthodoxy I would mean the
continuous historical development of the doctrine of Jesus and his apostles; and the orthodox habit or temper of mind I would consider
to be simply fidelity to the teachings of the
Spirit of Truth throughout Christian history,
as the things of Christ have been witnessed to

the church in its great confessions, and as the
words of the Lord are still opening their meanings, under new providential lights, in the enlarging thought of the Christian world. Orthodoxism, on the other hand, is the dogmatic
stagnation and ecclesiastical abuse of orthodoxy. Orthodoxism is an orthodoxy which has
ceased to grow—a dried and brittle orthodoxy.
Orthodoxism offers a crust of dogma kept over
from another century; it fails to receive the
daily bread for which we are taught this day
to pray. It has been my desire, therefore,
throughout these discourses, to represent, so
truthfully as I may, the orthodox spirit and belief—only not the orthodoxy of yesterday, but
of to-day.

It should be remembered that the first of these
discourses was intended for the relief of a popular prejudice against all creeds, and the reasoning
pursued should be judged with reference to the
object which I had immediately in view; if I
had been called to address upon the same topic
an ecclesiastical assembly, my growing conviction of our need of a revised theology, suited to

our scientific environment, and fitted to survive
in modern thought, would have led me to lay
the stress of my argument even more strongly
upon the desirability of a restatement of the
standards, particularly of my own, the Presbyterian church; and the conservatism usually
audible in such assemblies would have relieved
me from the necessity of pleading that justice
be done the old and hallowed forms of faith,
while urging timely preparation for the coming
of another of the days of the Son of man.

The view of the Atonement which is suggested in the third discourse seems to me to be
in harmony with the truth of Christ seen and
welcomed by many minds who have been awakened, by the touch of Dr. Bushnell's magic
thought, to simpler and more purely moral conceptions of the work of Christ; while, at the
same time, the Cross is regarded as in some real
sense necessary for the self-satisfaction of God's
own nature in forgiving sin; and therefore I
shall not, I trust, be found to have missed
wholly the truth hidden in the heart of the
older, sacrificial theology.

My dealing with current objections of popular scepticism would have been singularly incomplete without some endeavor, at least, on
my part to wrestle with the acknowledged difficulties of our belief in a future life of rewards
and punishments. My reasonings and conclusions upon these momentous questions may seem
to some too cautious and hesitating; others
whose minds are darkened under the shadow
of the awful possibilities of the retributive
government of God, may possibly be helped
by them to wait and trust; I can only say of
them that I have gone as far as I think reason
and the Scripture allow us to go with unhesitating feet, and I have stopped, and am waiting
for more light, where a step farther would
seem to me to be a step beyond the limits of
revelation—a doubtful leap which orthodox
theology should not push faith to take in the
dark.

To the discussion of the doctrine of the
future life I have added a sermon upon Social
Immortality, without which one chief element
of the hope of immortality would have been

left untouched. It may, also, help to swell the needed and growing reaction against that exaggerated and extreme individualism which has been at once the strength and the weakness of Protestantism, both the truth and the sophism of Calvinistic philosophy.

A few critical notes have been appended, in order to indicate more definitely, at some important points, the relation of positions assumed in the discourses to existing questions and beliefs.

These discourses, without further preface, I would introduce simply as one series of a pastor's working sermons; they are not sent forth under "the philosopher's cloak," but clothed in the working-dress of the ordinary ministration of the Word, and for the purpose of helping among men the removal of some common difficulties in the way of the coming of a better day of faith.

QUINCY, ILL., June, 1881.

DISCOURSES.

I.

THE CHURCHES AND CREEDS.

Nevertheless, whereto we have already attained, let us walk by the same rule, let us mind the same thing.—PHIL. iii. 16.

WE are told that the creeds of the churches are obstacles in the way of Christianity. If the doctrines upon which, as it is often, but incorrectly said, the churches are founded, should be removed, men would flock into them, and they would be filled to overflowing. But though in not a few churches creeds have been taken out of the way, the logic of facts has hardly justified the expectations of those who would banish them, and in no creedless church has Christianity come to its kingdom. I would not form a generalization from isolated facts, but the whole history of the church seems to show that the flow and power of a progressive Christianity has kept within certain general limits of belief, and that, too far beyond those limits, both churches and individuals lose the deep, strong current of the divine influence in human history. The repeated failures of attempts to build churches upon a basis of pure individualism, and the incontestable fact that Christianity has made steady progress along the lines of certain common beliefs and historical confessions, are reasons sufficient, at least, to prevent us from dismissing these creeds with an impatient gesture, as though we had only to bow them out in order to bow the world into the church.

I have spent many delightful hours of my life in the woods, but I have never seen a tree that had grown up through the storms—I have never noticed a single living twig—which nature had not provided with a covering of bark. A creedless church is like a barkless tree. The bark, it is true, should grow with the growth of the tree; but some bark seems to be a necessity of growth. Some creed is essential to the development of Christianity. I have looked down through the microscope into the first beginnings of life, and seen at the very bottom of all existence a mass of protoplasmic pulp; but the cell which is the unit of growth, the unit of the forming tissues, is a nucleus of life protected by an envelope, or wall, of formed matter. This analogy of natural growth will hardly mislead us in the higher spheres of mind and morals. Some formed matter, some fixed beliefs, would seem to be necessities of the growth of religion. Some creed—I am not speaking just now of its contents—is necessary to the mental growth of individuals. Christianity would be singularly incomplete did it not furnish materials for reason to fashion into systems of thought; and the intellectual completeness of Christianity has been to many profound intellects one of the evidences of its divine origin.

Some creed, moreover, some fixed idea of conduct, is necessary to the growth of character. We are not beyond the wisdom of the proverb, "As he thinketh in his heart"—that is, as a man really believes—"so is he."

Some creed is still more a social necessity, essential to the existence and perpetuity of the new society which it is the distinctive glory of Christianity to have called forth. Jesus came preaching the kingdom of God. His object from the first was not simply to call the individual disciple to follow him, but to create an apostolic fellowship; not merely to save the individual soul, but to save it for a society of the redeemed. The new, higher society created in this world by Jesus, affords, by its existence and perpetuity, one of the distinctive and characteristic evidences of his supernatural virtue. Christianity issues, as no other religion so naturally and so powerfully, in a church. But this new society is and must be a fellowship in the truth. The doctrine of Jesus, therefore, as it was received by the apostles, and as it opens its manifold meanings with the growth of Christian thought, is not only to be regarded as an essential part of Christianity, but also as one of its first social necessities.

Most men, therefore, may agree with me that some creed is a necessity required by the very nature of mind and morals, and indispensable

to the upbuilding of a higher Christian society.
Their objections to creeds, however, really lie
against their contents or their abuses. I shall
refer, therefore, to several objections of this
description against our present forms or administration of Christianity. I would not, however, take up these objections in any spirit of
controversy, for I have noticed that when men
begin to debate, truth usually begins to suffer;
but there are doubts and difficulties concerning our creeds which sometimes find expression
in our popular literature, which ought to be
frequently and fairly weighed by the orthodox
clergy, and which, so far as they may be found
to spring not entirely from our mistaking Jesus'
method, but from some misapprehension of our
real intentions in the administration of Christ's
church, or from popular prejudices resting upon
half truths, we should spare no pains to remove
or correct.

The first objection which has recently been
brought to our attention, is that the churches
have a "tendency to repress free thought," and
that "no progress has been made in theology."
I ask first of all, whether statements such as

these, though now frequently alleged, are wholly in accordance with the facts? A tendency is a long-continued movement, not always to be determined by the apparent direction of the moment. We must not judge the sweep of a mountain range by the foothills; we should not measure the trend of the coast by the little inlet upon whose shore we may dwell. Estimated by any large historic judgment, determined by any fair observation of the present condition of theological studies, I venture to affirm that it is not true that the churches have a tendency to repress free thought. But I may be asked: Do you forget Col. Ingersoll's array of thumb-screws? No: I do not forget them, nor the labored and ingenious unfairness of Prof. Draper's book upon the "Conflict between Religion and Science." In any scientific test, however, we should determine the invariable antecedents of any given phenomenon, if we would discover its true cause. If we study the history of intolerance in a truly scientific method, and not ourselves under the influence of some narrowing prejudice, we shall find that persecutions and bigotry have flourished not only in the heated

air of a tropical religious fervor, but also under
the arctic chill of stoic coldness; not only within
the pale of Christian faith, but also amid the
most opposite beliefs, and even in the domain of
science; and that, under all forms, and everywhere, the invariable antecedents, the ultimate
causes, of intolerance and persecution are certain
natural limitations of men's minds, certain evil
propensities of human nature, and bad passions of
men's hearts. Some beliefs, it is true, may lend
themselves more easily than others to the abuse
of blind prejudice, and as some of the brightest
virtues may be shadowed by the darkest faults,
so there are noblest truths which may be turned
to the basest uses. But many of the faults of
Christians, and many evils to be deplored in the
churches, I would cite rather as evidences of one
of the fundamental doctrines of the church—the
sad corruption of human nature, and our need
of regeneration by a purer and divine Spirit.
"What drives poetry out of the world?" asked
Goethe; and he answered, "The poets." "What
drives Christianity out of the world?" it might
be asked, and we might answer, "The Christians." But, in either case, a clever satire should

not be mistaken for a sober, historical judgment.

I am not contented, however, with a merely
apologetic or negative answer to this objection.
I reply again, that on the whole it does not seem
to be true that the churches have repressed free
thought. I will not dwell now upon their general service to liberty. The lawgiver of old,
coming from the presence of the Great King to
stand before an earthly monarch, to bid him let
a whole people go free, was a true prototype
and image of the mission through the centuries
of the religion of the Bible. But I wish to give
a more specific answer to the objection. I affirm
that these very creeds of the church themselves
were the results of progressive thought, and
marked epochs of free inquiry. They are
the high-water marks of great movements of
thought. That earliest of the general creeds,
the Nicene, had three centuries of thought
behind it. Three centuries of mental wrestling
with the greatest problems of human thought,
three centuries of free discussion by awakened
and earnest minds, stand behind that creed.
Let any man here do as I was once required to

do in the class-room of a theological seminary, follow the course of the growth of that creed, from mind to mind and from age to age; let him seek so to enter into and understand the thought finally issuing in that creed, as to be able to pass an examination upon it; and, I venture to suggest, he will find that he has subjected himself to no easy mental discipline, and he will feel himself, at least, debarred henceforth from speaking of the creeds of the churches as the work of "blind belief," of "ignorant and superstitious ages."

The same remark holds true of our great Protestant confessions of faith. They were born in liberty. They were wrought out in free discussion. They have passed through the fire. They were the work of men in whose souls were ringing the words with which Luther awoke Germany in his address to the "Christian Nobility," and whose hearts were vibrating to his lofty strain in his sermon on "The Freedom of the Christian Man." These words of confession "have drawn transcendent meanings up" from the lives of martyrs. When I can take my little boy to the State capitol, and bid him laugh at the tattered flags, torn to shreds, upon which are written the names of great battle-fields of freedom, and which brave hands and loyal hearts once bore through the battle's storm, —then, but not till then, can I speak aught but words of reverence and gratitude for the symbols of faiths so nobly realized as these confessions which have come to us from out the great conflicts of the ages—faiths which have been borne aloft as banners by heroic spirits—creeds which martyrs have sealed with blood!

But, it may be said, we admit that these creeds were once wrought out in liberty, but have they not since become oppressive? It is true that in literature, in art, in civilization, a great creative age is usually followed by an age of formalism and stagnation. Theology is not exempt from this general law of human progress. The creative theology of the Reformation was succeeded by a period of pause and dogmatism. In the seventeenth century a Protestant legalism and a Protestant traditionalism sprang up and threatened to overgrow the theology of the Reformation. Something of that tendency to embalm faith safely in confessionalism may possibly still linger, and manifest itself occasionally, in a stiff, pulseless orthodoxism; but the spirit of seventeenth century dogmatism is certainly not the spirit of the living orthodox theology of to-day. The late Prof. Bagehot, in his bright little book on "Physics and Politics," remarks that one of the first necessities for a savage tribe becoming civilized, is to gain a "legal fibre," a "crust of custom." And the next necessity, he says, may be to break up that crust. The growth of Christianity may not be free from this general condition of progress. But Christianity has shown wonderful power in breaking up its own crusts. They are breaking up now. The ice is going out. The primal Christian faiths are not departing; never fear that they shall be swept away! But every form that is in the way of true religious progress, every crust which is no longer useful, Christianity *in* the churches is preparing to break up.

Neither is it true that at the present time our creeds are generally used repressively as conditions of membership in the church. Has any member of this church, as a condition of admission to its fellowship, ever been asked to subscribe to the Westminster Confession? There may be instances where good men have been kept by doctrinal obstructions from the Lord's table, but they are rare, and happily are becoming rarer. Why, two hundred years ago, in that denomination which traces back its faith to the same general historical confessions which we follow, in the Cambridge platform of the Congregational churches, it was expressly written that in the examination of candidates for admission to the church "a rational charity" should be exercised, and "the weakest measure of faith" should be accepted.

If any man wishes to be known as a disciple of the Lord Jesus Christ, to confess him, and to keep his commandments; if he is willing to come humbly and sincerely as a disciple, and in the spirit of a disciple; let him knock and see whether any orthodox church, in any intelligent Christian community, will now turn him aside, even though he be weak in the faith, before he complains that our long creeds are put in the way between him and the Master; and then, if he should be rejected, I am not the only orthodox clergyman who would stand with him outside the church, if needs must be, for the principle of Christian liberty!

Though our creeds are not now generally abused as conditions of church-membership, we are reproached, however, on account of the restrictions placed by most evangelical bodies upon their clergy; it is said that they are "not free to express their honest convictions." If that is the fact, I have happily been unconscious of it. I have not, up to the present hour, found my liberty to think under the law of truth—and that is the only freedom an honest mind can desire—abridged, or interfered with, in the church. It is true that there are still to be found in some churches a few theological Nimrods who are mighty hunters before the Lord, and the beginnings of whose kingdom is Babel. It is true, also, in any of our denominations, that if a man brings to them a contentious spirit, he will very likely receive of the same measure which he gives. If he begins his ministry with the sword, he will probably perish by the sword, and he ought to perish by the sword! But if any man does, to-day, honest, constructive work;

2

if he tries to bring to this generation the truths of God which it needs, he may hope to find friends springing up all around him, to receive words of encouragement from brave men in all the churches, and to meet with scholarly criticism even from seats of conservatism.[1]

"Yes," it will be said, "but there stands the Westminster Confession, gloomy and forbidding —what will you say of that?" It does not stand as a prison-house in which any of us are shut up. The system of philosophy which was built up into that confession we are not compelled to accept. But, if you admit that its language is moss-grown, and its philosophy antiquated, why do you not at once remove or revise it? I might answer with truthfulness that a historical confession, historically interpreted, may possibly afford larger liberty than could be enjoyed under a modern confession legally interpreted. But more than this needs to be said. Our "Confession of Faith" is under revision at the present time. It is under revision in every intelligent sermon in every thoughtful Presbyterian pulpit. It is under revision in every live Presbyterian seminary, and in every good Presbyterian paper. Moreover, within the memory of this generation, the Westminster Confession has been factually revised—revised in fact, if not in form. Thanks to the fathers, many of whom are still living, such a revision took place in the admission of the New England, or New School, theology into full recognition in the reunited Presbyterian church; and that revision, real, if not formal, is my warrant —and it is the sufficient warrant for any ministers whose are the fathers, but whose faces are turned toward the future—for occupying in good conscience a Presbyterian pulpit.

Still it may be asked, why not bring at once your ecclesiastical standards into line with the more enlightened theology of the church? I answer again, creeds are not to be made in a day. They are necessarily of slow growth. Many of us may think the old house needs to be rebuilt; some of its chambers may be too narrow, some of the ceilings too low; but we do not mean to move our family until we are sure that the new house is thoroughly built and seasoned. We are not so impatient as to be willing to put green timber into its construction. We prefer to build of seasoned timber. Some question whether this is a creed-building age. There are still open questions upon which we are looking for more light. There are results of modern investigations to be thoroughly sifted and tried. Let the work of formal revision of our standards go on and be brought to completion as speedily as it may. Many of us will rejoice in that day, and are indeed straitened in mind until that good work be accomplished. But we are more anxious to do the real work of revision, to adjust our own faiths happily to modern conditions of thought, and to learn to preach them in the new tongues of knowledge, than we are impatient to record the results of our labors in the organic law or constitution of our church. So long as that law is not used oppressively; so long as we have accorded to us the liberty of Christ in the church; we will seek first, as far as the truth may shine before us and lead us on, to do the real work of revision, and be content to leave the results to time. Conflicts, indeed, may yet arise for liberty within the church, as they have in the past. Then the hour will find the men. But conflicts shall not be precipitated by any impatience of ours. True reform cannot be wrought in an hour; the great base of the advancing wave does not move so fast as the curling crest which breaks into foam upon the beach. Reformed creeds come not in a moment, but they are always only questions of time. The best thought in all Christian denominations is at work simplifying, elevating, reforming our theology; lifting the whole body of it up into a purer ethical light; and we can wait in hope; we shall have revised confessions of our faith, if not to-day, perhaps to-morrow.

This whole objection, therefore, that our churches and our creeds stand in the way of free Christian thought—thought loyal to Christian truth—seems to be at the present time, to a very large extent at least, an anachronism— an objection which, as somewhat out of date and really behind the times, may be deemed outlawed in any court of large, reasonable judgment of present facts and tendencies.

It has been urged, however, that theology has made no progress. Here, also, I would join issue upon the facts, and reply that theology has made great and gratifying progress; and I will give the following specifications that my assertion may not be left indefinite: (1.) Theology has made progress in its methods. There are theologians who have been quick to avail themselves of improved scientific and historical methods of inquiry. It costs moie now, more time and more study, than it did formerly to obtain a good theological education. One must receive a broader and more varied training to be held now in any repute among theologians. (2.) Theology has made progress in its language. The natural language for the expression of spiritual truths has been greatly enhanced by our sciences. Nature was never so rich a parable of the kingdom of heaven. Any one familiar with our best current theological literature is sensible of this freshness and new power of expression which spiritual thought is receiving from natural science. (3.) Theology has made progress along the lines of certain great doctrines, among which I will specify these: our idea of God, and the relation of the natural to the supernatural; our conception of the Person and the work of Christ, and our view of the future life. These particulars will form the subject of subsequent discourses.

I pass now to a second general objection to our creeds recently urged among us, one often felt, too, by believers as well as by unbelievers. Difficulty is found in the fact that the Christian doctrines, as commonly received, transcend experience and contain mysteries. "Nothing which is revealed," it is popularly urged, "can be mysterious." What? A revelation cannot be mysterious! But the very day is a mystery of light which, with all our science, we cannot understand. Can there be no partial revelations, no progressive revelation? Are there not realities coming for a moment within the dim horizons of our consciousness—realities more felt than seen? "Nothing which is revealed can be mysterious!" One needs only to dwell amid the daily revelations of a Christian home to know that there are verities of affection believed in with all the heart, love which

> "My soul can reach, when feeling out of sight
> For the ends of Being and Ideal Grace,"

the depth and breadth and height of which eternity only can comprehend. "Just so far as the

Bible is a revelation," we are assured, "just so
far it ceases to be mysterious." That reasoning
which is so often urged against the Christian
doctrine, is at best only a half truth; it needs
to be completed with this truth—just so far as
the Bible is a revelation it will bring to light
mysteries still to be revealed. This common
difficulty with revelation on account of its mysteries is an instance of the frequent fallacy of
suppressing the minor premise in our thinking.
The objection urged is true only according to
the idea of revelation which is left unquestioned
and unmentioned in the reasoning; but that is
the very idea that needs to be determined. Towards the close of the last century a system of
philosophy was built upon this idea that only
those things are true which can be clearly understood. But the period of "Illuminism" in
Germany proved to be shallow and transient,
and this philosophy of wisdom without mysteries bore very much the same relation to the
real life of reason that a Japanese picture, without light or shade, bears to a painting of Rem-
brandt. Every science reveals mysteries. You
cannot talk to your child about your own life

in the world without exciting his wonder by your words. Every light brings to view the larger circle of darkness. What is knowledge but a growing wonder? No revelation, then, of a future life could be given to us which would not leave even more than it discloses in shadow and mystery. We should remember that perplexities which we often feel with regard to the future life—the burden of questions which we cannot lift—are occasioned by the very fact that we do have some faith in immortality, and that Christianity has opened to us some revelation of the hereafter.

Having thus pointed out the evident fallacy in this popular objection against the doctrines of faith because they contain mysteries, I should do work very unsatisfactory to myself, at least, if I did not hasten to point out the truth, also, which is in it. For there is a truth underlying this reasoning of doubt. A revelation which contains mysteries, and in many respects transcends experience, must have, at least, some points of contact with human reason, and in part it will verify and confirm itself in human experience. This is precisely what the religion

2*

of the Bible does. It finds us in our truest
human experiences. If I am reading a book of
travels and find the descriptions trustworthy of
places where I have been, and of scenes with
which I am familiar, I may give credence to the
writer when he describes countries which I have
never visited, or narrates events unlike any which
I may have witnessed. This is Jesus' own argument for his authority in declaring truths which
transcend our little experience : "If I have told
you earthly things and ye believe not, how shall
ye believe if I tell you of heavenly things?"
Because we can and have verified revelation in
those teachings in which it does submit itself to
reason, conscience, and the proof of experience,
we believe it, also, in those heavenly teachings
which transcend our understandings, and of
which Jesus has many things to say, but not
now.

Those who object to the churches on account
of their creeds remind us sometimes, and with
reason, that we should prefer above all things,
the "spiritual teachings" of Jesus. But let us
take care not to play fast and loose with the
meaning of words. The word spiritual is rich

and comprehensive. It implies that we are
spirits; that there is a side of human nature
turned toward the unseen; that the soul, itself
an unseen presence, has some relation to the Invisible; that there is a Father of spirits. The
spiritual teachings of Jesus comprise more than
our mere human duties or moral conduct; they
involve our religious position and bearing, our
obligations to God, our relations, right or wrong,
towards God. But still more than this is com-
prehended in these teachings. Christianity is
not a mere philosophy; it is a spirit of life, em-
bodied in historical fact. It is a divine Spirit
living, breathing, among men, actuating and in-
spiring a chosen people, its organ and means of
revelation—the Spirit given at last without
measure to the Christ in whom all the law and
the prophets were fulfilled. The spiritual teachings of Jesus involve, therefore, his teaching
concerning the work of God in the history of
the chosen people, and concerning his own Person and life as a revelation in the form of man
of the glory of the Father; in short, his whole
doctrine of the kingdom of God already come,
and to come, on earth. These " spiritual teach-

ings " of Jesus in their comprehensiveness the
churches seek in their confessions of faith to
embrace and to interpret.

We would not, then, be understood to hold
our creeds as perfect ecclesiastical fortifications,
or even as complete statements of theological
truth. Revelation, like nature, is larger than
our largest knowledge of it, and whenever one
finishes his system of thought, and closes up all
its definitions, he is sure to have left some truth
out. We would leave, at least, on every side of
our spiritual heritage, gates open into the undis-
covered country—those realms of life and light
which stretch beyond our present horizons; but
while we would not shut ourselves up in dogmatic exclusiveness,—while we would keep the
windows open for any ray of light to stream in,
or for any birds of passage to pour in upon us
their songs from the skies,—we rejoice that we
are not left by the God of the Bible without
shelter and houseless, to wander in orphanage of
spirit, without country or home. There are
truths old and familiar, at whose friendly hearth
we have learned to rest and to wait; there are
some faiths, tried and sure, in which, as did

our fathers before us, we can live and would die.

But if, after all that has been said, any one should still ask, why not, in view of the admitted difficulties of doctrine and creed, suffer us to live contented with the simple, moral precepts of Jesus, I will answer that question when any man can tell me if he has ever seen a field of wheat growing and ripening without any expanse of sky over it? The grain cannot mature without a sky. There can be no perfect morality without some chemistry of the heavens in it. Every life needs some sky. Every man, we urge, has a larger life to live than that part of it which is turned towards this world or one's fellow men. Religion is morality towards God. A man's real creed is his working-theory of life. The churches seek, by their doctrines, however far short of the spiritual teachings of Jesus they may fall, to present to men the largest and best working-theory of life. We would warn the young against partial and defective working-theories of life. We would preach the Gospel of Christ as the one sufficient, and complete, and tried, working-theory of life.

II.

God is love.—1st JOHN, iv. 16.

IF one should pursue in the pulpit, with pains-taking thought, the line of reasoning which the Christian scholarship of to-day regards as commanding the lower lines of materialism and modern scepticism, he would very probably be met with the reproach that he was evading the objections which are popularly urged against the Bible, and the difficulties which are still lying unremoved in the minds of the people. I think that is true, and I am glad that it is true. The best Christian scholarship does evade the common troubles of popular infidelity as a traveller up an Alpine pass evades the fogs and the mists which lie in the valleys beneath. The Christian scholarship of the present day does escape the difficulties upon which an In-

gersoll expects faith to make shipwreck of itself,
as the mariner avoids the shoals and the break-
ers on the coast, who has the courage to spread
his sails to the airs of heaven, and chooses the
breadth and freedom of the ocean for his heritage.

Having already considered some objections
which are popularly raised against the manner
in which our creeds are held in the churches;
having urged their necessary uses, while admit-
ting that a progressive church, led by the Spirit
of Christ, must always keep its historical confessions under the process of revision and adap-
tation to new environments of thought; I have
now to enter upon a somewhat larger field of
discussion, and to take up the question which
we ought fairly to consider, whether the orthodox theology of the present hour stands in the
way of faith. We should be willing, in the in-
terest of truth, and of faith as well, to review
at any time our own positions, to search our own
creeds, to satisfy ourselves whether, in the contents of our beliefs, there is anything which can
justly be subjected to the charge of being a
hindrance to spiritual faith among thoughtful
and honest minds. In such review and revi-

sion of our beliefs, I do not, however, feel called upon to answer old objections, often urged, against the Latin or Calvinistic theology. I am to speak simply for what I regard as the orthodox theology of to-day. Are its beliefs oppressive to moral reason, or difficulties in the way of spiritual thought?

The particular class of doubts and misgivings concerning our theology which I would consider this evening, may be fairly summarized, I think, in this single sentence: Orthodoxy is charged with misunderstanding and misrepresenting God. This is certainly a most serious charge, and one which orthodoxy should be ready earnestly and humbly to weigh. Of all beings God has been most misunderstood—misrepresented by many who have not wished to do his will, and misunderstood ofttimes in the bosoms of his chosen friends. It is a coarse, and yet too common remark that the creed of the churches " sets up a demon in the place of God "—a being who " conforms more nearly to our idea of a devil than of a God."

There is one thing with regard to this reproach so often cast upon our theology which I

can say without any fear of contention : should
any person seek for admission into this, or any
other evangelical church, and say, "I am willing to confess faith in your creeds—I will believe your doctrines—though they make God
seem to me to be a terrible being, like a demon ;" our answer would be prompt and decisive, No! we will not accept such a confession! Let God be true, though every man be a
liar! We do not want you so to believe, so to
understand, our creeds, as to make the church
to you a place of devil-worship. Rather would
we have you come in as a little child, knowing
only that you have a heart that needs God, a
heart that needs divine mercy and forgiveness,
than have you stand here and confess with your
lips our systems of divinity, if their meaning to
you should darken the heavens, or rob your
own conscience of its sense of the truth and
beauty of the Lord.

But more than this might be said. It might
be shown that the whole history of the orthodox conception of God, from the first century
until now, has been the history of a progressive
idea. The revelation which began in the He-

brew fear of the Lord God Almighty, and which was finished in the manifestation of God in the person of Christ—the completed revelation of God in the Bible—arose, at length, upon a world full of false ideas of deity, into whose atmosphere, laden with emanations of evil, it shone, burning up the fogs, sometimes, indeed, itself overclouded, but always breaking through the clouds, and filling the whole world more and more with the knowledge and glory of God.

Leaving, however, this possible historical justification of the idea of God which has been growing in Christian theology, I wish rather to ask whether the idea of God now cherished in the representative minds of representative churches, is justly liable to this reproach of morally misunderstanding God. On the contrary it seems to me that the representative evangelical theology of the present day is availing itself reverently, yet boldly, of the best methods of growing in the knowledge of God.

It is not with men in general a question, must we worship? but whom, and how? We might almost assert that there are no confessed, educated atheists at the present day. For science does not say, "There is no God;" but, "I cannot see; I do not know." The great question is, can God be known? and orthodoxy, instead of degrading man's being, and regarding the moral nature as a paralytic to the touch of divine influences, affirms that the spirit which is in man can and does respond to the energy, in its own thought and life, of the Spirit of God; that man is capable of some real, though partial, knowledge of God; that the reason and the conscience are the organs of spiritual apprehension through which man looks up into the very nature of deity. You will find the orthodoxy of to-day asserting in the schools of philosophy, as well as before the people, the fact that man has a spiritual birthright, that in every beat of his heart, in every thought which he thinks, he can, and he does, know something about God.

Orthodoxy, then, honors the reason and the conscience as the organs of spiritual knowledge. It finds a higher power at the fountains of our moral and religious consciousness; and all rational thought is the outflowing, or development, of the divine life which is in us, and of the divine truth revealed to the spirit in man, of which all visible things are the metaphors and expression.

But this is not all. Our Christian theology not only avails itself of these natural means of knowing God—means of spiritual apprehension which have not been wholly lost or destroyed by the terrific, blinding power of sin; but Christian theology remembers, also, with grateful recognition, this great truth of God, "He first loved us," and it would, therefore, accept the providences in which that Love, before our thought of God, has sought to make itself known among men, and it would look up to the mysteries of God, and study the thoughts of God toward us, through a historic revelation.

But here I strike upon one of the strongest objections that has ever been made against Christian theology. I will not state it to you in the imperfect and more easily answered form in which it lies before me in a popular presentation of it; for I think there is a real difficulty here which should be fairly met, and I will bring it before you in the form in which it has entered into the history of modern thought, in

its strongest and most formidable presentation.
I shall read to you Lessing's famous reason for
his disbelief in historical Christianity, for I wish
to show that Orthodoxy at least is honest, and
will keep nothing back; that there are Christian ministers in Christian pulpits who prefer,
when occasion offers, not to take advantage of
imperfect popular statements of objections to
their faith, but to deal honestly and fairly with
those objections in their strongest and best
forms.

"If no historical truth can be demonstrated,"
wrote Lessing, "then, also, can nothing be demonstrated through historical truths. That is,
accidental truths of history cannot be the evidence of necessary truths of reason." That is
the brightest and best thing that rationalism
has ever said. It presents the most serious difficulty which philosophic doubt can raise against
a simple historical faith in Christianity. "This,"
says Lessing, continuing his argument that
truths such as the received belief in Christianity
affirms, cannot be demonstrated by truths which
are only historically certain, "This is the foul,
broad ditch over which I cannot come, often

and earnestly as I have made the spring. Can any one help me over? Let him do it, I entreat him; I adjure him!"

Providence was already leading the church over that chasm between historical and spiritual faith which Lessing found unbridged by the theology of his day. The practical answer, as has been well said, which Providence gave to rationalism was Moravianism and Methodism. Through the historical gospel of the life and work of Jesus, souls became filled with a new sense of God, and aglow with the light of the Spirit;—the Spirit of truth and of power used these facts of the gospel history as the chosen means of its own work of saving souls.

Providence gave, also, as the philosophical answer to Lessing's reluctant rationalism, a profounder and a purer theology than Lessing found in the orthodoxism of his day—a theology which has searched the depths of Christian consciousness, and which has found in Christian life and experience the present and immediate evidence of the religion of the Bible. This revivified theology sees in Christianity not simply a Christ-idea, but a Christ-fact in the world, and it finds the real and commanding evidence of that divine fact in humanity in its present and continuous power, in its living energy and spiritual efficacy, in the consciousness of believers. Experience proves that when a mind is brought into vital contact with historical Christianity, with the facts of the gospel of Jesus Christ, that mind at once, and as though a new and divine energy had touched it, expands and rises to enlarged and purified conceptions of God.

Thus a boy in Japan once found a leaf of the Bible—a simple, bare record of historical fact. But it led him across the ocean in search of the Christian's God. He learned our language, and, as historical Christian records were brought to his knowledge, just as any other book might have been brought, his mind seemed to pass through what was almost a new creation; it rose to such conceptions of the Deity as it had never before imagined—the witness of the Spirit within confirmed the record of God given in the historical gospel; and that boy, become now a Christian man, has gone back to Japan a missionary of the Cross of Christ, and has lived to see his own parents destroy their idols under the influence of the same historical testimony to God in Christ. This, I say, is what historical Christianity has done thousands of times in bringing to men knowledge of the true God—that knowledge which is eternal life.

The vast difference between a merely moral or ideal belief in God and that knowledge of God which is given and assured in Christian experience through God revealed in Christ, may perhaps be made visible by a simple illustration. Suppose a child to have lost its parents in infancy, and to have been carried to another country and brought up among strangers who never had known them. That child might gain, as he grew of age, a theoretical, but not a personal, knowledge of what it is to have a mother and father. He would come to know these first, best facts of human experience by inference and deduction, but from no real vital experience of them, as the child cradled in love, and growing up in a happy Christian home, knows them by heart, and can never forget them in the after years, wherever he may wander. Such is the difference between natural and revealed religion—between a faith in God de-

pendent upon philosophical conclusions, and a
real experience of God manifest in Christ. Our
Christian faith is the experience of the man who
has been brought up from childhood in the
Father's house. For God revealed himself of
old, in the childhood of humanity, as the one
supreme authority and guide, the law of human
history. He gave commandments, promises,
warnings, through holy men inspired by the
Holy Ghost. The Word came and dwelt among
us in the form of man. He has lived—the
Lord has lived—a divine life upon this earth,
with us, and for us—a life of God in our human history and through history! "My Father
worketh hitherto, and I work." God has not
remained beyond the stars, unknown and at an
infinite distance. He has been present as a
divine fact and a divine power among men,
present in the supernatural development of that
religion whose supreme and final revelation is a
sinless life, and a character unique and peerless,
through which is declared the very glory of the
Father. Therefore we say, we have more than
a religion of ideas; ours is a better confession
of faith than that; we have a religion of what

God has done for us; a religion of historical facts, which are full of the glory and praise of the Father; a religion which, upon the foundation which is laid deep in the earthliness and sinfulness of our history, rises to heights of Christian experience around which still shines the light of the love of God. So the past fact of Christ in history becomes the present truth of the Spirit of Christ in human hearts.

Many who seem ready to cast loose from historical Christianity would retain their belief in the fatherhood of God and the brotherhood of man. But do they not know that those very beliefs came through these historical channels, came borne to earth upon these historical facts? that what no pagan philosophy had ever succeeded in accomplishing was historically wrought into the character of a chosen people? and that Christianity, the outcome of the religion of the Bible, first bore to a world of bending slaves and woman, degraded and forlorn, these great faiths, which are our Christian heritage—the fatherhood of God and the brotherhood of man?[2]

To sum up, then, the result, so far, of my

reasoning, orthodoxy, I would claim, avails itself of the best methods of knowing God, viz.,
conscience and reason, and historical revelation.
I may go still farther, and assert that, partial
and unworthy as we must confess are our best
thoughts of God, nevertheless, our progressive
orthodoxy has gained, and is growing in, the
most purely moral conception of God which can
be found anywhere in this world.

In this direction there has been great and
gratifying progress since the reformation. Remember that the reformers brought, and it was
necessary that they should bring to their world,
this truth : that God is Lord, alone is King. By
two revolutionary truths—truths which came to
them through a historical revelation—Luther
and Calvin changed the face of modern civilization. Luther rose up in the freedom of the
Christian man against a soul-enslaving power,
and proclaimed the doctrine of justification by
faith. John Calvin stood over against that great
world-enslaving power, the power of the papacy,
which was assuming God's throne on earth, and
proclaimed—there is only one King, one Lord,
whose government not only controls nations, but

whose decree, also, reaches down beneath individual liberty, and upholds all things by its infrustrable power;—and by that mighty truth of divine sovereignty Calvin and the reformers did what infidelity has never done, what a thousand Ingersolls could never do, sounded forth a triumphant peal for the liberty of the souls of men, and set the modern nations free. It is to Calvinism, more than to any other single power, that the modern State owes its liberty; and, though we may have found a larger life and a higher thought of God than our fathers knew, there is a needed reproof for any who would belie the spiritual parentage of our laws and liberties in the old and homely proverb, "It is an ill bird that fouls its own nest."

Orthodoxy has accomplished more than Calvinism began to do. Progressive orthodoxy has reached a higher conception of the Godhead than it was permitted the Calvinistic reformers to gain. For Calvinism, as it confronted the great despotism over souls with its sublime doctrine of the divine sovereignty, after all presented but a half-truth of divinity to men, and it had itself much of the Gospel still to learn.

Theologians, seizing its leading truth, worked it out to its extreme consequences, and we should be thankful that they did; for just as materialism, or Haeckelism, has shown that Darwinism, if carried to its extreme results, fails to give a complete solution of the problem of life, so Calvinism, logically worked out, carried to its extreme consequences, shows itself to be in need of Christ, in need of the Gospel of love, in need of being lifted bodily up into a higher, more ethically Christian conception of God, our Father in heaven. The chief want of Calvinistic confessions of faith is the play of the light and hope of the gospel over them. Their divine truths are left too much in the shadow of their human philosophy. A system of theology may be firmly constructed, and solid as a granitic formation; but if it is to be true to nature and the Bible, God's sunlight must not be shut out.

The reaction from Calvinistic theology at first tended toward the other extreme. Men began to chase the sunbeams and to lose firm footing on everlasting principles. After the reformers, by sterner truths, had gained men's liberty, their

descendants seemed disposed to enthrone a com-
plaisant good-nature, or a distant indifference,
as God; they remembered that the Lord is merciful, and they began to overlook the dark, world-
destroying power of sin. But orthodoxy, having learned something of its own earlier fatal-
istic error, but avoiding this other humanitarian
extreme, went on to work out from nature, the
human heart, and the Bible, its own truth of
the Godhead; and I have before me a book
that has just come from the press, in which the
greatest living theologian, Prof. Dorner, has
gathered up the ripe fruit of his theological
studies, and I find there such conceptions of God
in the completeness of his attributes and fulness
of his love, as make both mind and heart rejoice
in the glory of the Lord. Where else in the
whole field of theological literature can be
found nobler, worthier, more thoroughly ethical
conceptions of God than the orthodox theology
of to-day is giving through its living masters?
Escaping the limitations both of Calvinism and
humanitarianism, it would have us worship God
as infinitely majestic, and holy, and yet unspeakably beautiful and attractive. God is

love. This is the Christian philosophy of God, working itself out through the centuries, freed from the corruptions of Paganism, and clearing itself, also, from the shadows of scholastic theology. God is love—love which itself is a trinity, the unity of three primitive rays divine. For love, in the one ray or primal color of it, is benevolence—the giving of self for another's good; and love is, also, sympathy—the putting self in place of another, living another's life, the vicariousness of the cross; and love is also self-respect—the unselfish assertion of its own worth, the preservation of its own good in the world. Benevolence, vicariousness, righteousness, form the three-fold nature of love, which itself is a unity of life. God is love; love which includes all his attributes—mercy, sympathy, goodness, justice—all that can enter into the nature of a perfect and adorable Deity, so that the very omnipotence of God is itself an attribute of love, and with the wisdom of God serves always his love. "Love," insists Prof. Dorner, "is the power in God over his own omnipotence." If we once rise freely and exultingly to this thoroughly evangelical conception of God, we shall find that we are above and beyond many of the difficulties and doubts which often perplex and imprison faith.[3]

Orthodoxy, then, takes its doctrines and the facts of nature, and thinks them out just so far as it can without coming in conflict with its own conception of God; and when it finds that it is coming into conflict with its own faith in God, it stops short in its reasonings, and bows its head, and hides its own questionings in the heart of its assured knowledge of the Love whom it adores. Predestination, election, all these objectionable doctrines, these "horrible doctrines"—what will orthodoxy do with them? The worst doctrine of election to-day is taught by our natural science. The scientific doctrine of natural selection is the doctrine of election robbed of all hope, and without a single touch of human pity in it. I blame not our science; it simply seeks to be true to the facts of law and life; it finds even in nature a continuous process of selection unbroken from the beginning until now; but while it holds that all things may possibly work together for some far off and larger good, it has not a single tear of

pity to let fall for the individual who may be
crushed beneath life's heavy load. What does
our theology—our "hard theology"—have to
say? It will not turn from the facts. Whatever else you may say of it, modern orthodoxy
is no coward! It has become used to the edge
of the precipice, it has looked down into the
depths, its ear is haunted with the sound of the
cataracts! It will look the facts in the face—
the fact of sin, the fact of divine law, the fact
of condemnation and death. But orthodoxy
does also what no science can do; it takes these
factssand holds them up before its clear, shining
faith that God is love. It takes these facts,
awful though they are, and brings them to
Jesus, and leaves them at the foot of the Cross.
Orthodoxy sees the chasms, and the precipices,
and the wild cataracts; but it sees, also, shed
abroad over all, the light of the love of God;
it would behold them no more under any cloud
of its own foolish imaginations, or heavy, over-
shadowing traditions; it would see them in the
sunlight of the Gospel, in the joy of its faith in
the perfect goodness of the perfect God. And
so, reserving many questions, as Erasmus once

3*

said they should be reserved, not until the next general council, but until that hour when we shall stand face to face with God, our theology has patience, and can wait. Having rested as a child upon the bosom of the infinite Fatherhood of God, our faith is content if it can feel close to its own trembling heart the beatings of that heart which is ever true and unchangeable in its goodness, even though it may be darkness and night round about it as it lies upon the bosom of God.

If, however, we are asked why should our theology trouble itself with thought about these high themes, the answer is, Christian theology cannot shirk; it must think out and work out, so far as it has power, under its own pure conception of God, these ever-present problems of human existence; and I reply again that the belief in God, the theology which we may gain and hold through all our questionings, is of most practical moment to us—the whole direction and conduct of life will be determined by it. Our theology is really the most practical concern of human life. The ancients had no true knowledge of the earth, as they had no just conception of the sun; so there must be some true idea of God in order that there may be any adequate understanding of man, his wants, his range of capabilities, and his destiny; and civilizations are made to differ by the ideas of God which shine over them, as they are clear and true, or clouded and corrupted. A man's theology enters as an essential element into his daily life. It does make a difference in the color of the life whether, when we awake in the morning and enter upon the duties of the day, we believe in God; whether, as we go forth to our work, we walk as seeing Him who is invisible; whether, when we return to our homes, we gather our families together and offer our prayer of thanksgiving and praise to our Father who is in heaven. It does make a difference in the complexion and tenor of the life whether we believe in God so that our hearts are not troubled or afraid; and it does make a difference, too, in the rightness of a man's character, whether he holds a true filial relation to the person of God; for, if God is love, capable, because he is love, of entering into personal relations with his creatures, then

there are duties which we owe to God—and one
duty cannot be made the substitute for another
duty.   Honesty in your business would not ex-
cuse you for a lack of patriotism, nor patriotism
for a want of kindness in your home; and if
there be a God, our Father and our Friend,
then, as we have duties toward one another, so,
also, there is a morality which we owe to God.
Christ, then, was right when he said, "Seek ye
first the kingdom of God and His righteousness"—that righteousness which is the sanction
of every human duty, the inspiration of every
moral enthusiasm, the security of true affection,
the peace, the joy, the eternal life of the soul.

III.

In the sixteenth verse of the third chapter of the Gospel of John is this word from Jesus—it must have been a revelation from Jesus, for no human mind ever could have invented it, no human heart ever would have dreamed of it, it could only have proceeded from a divinely filled consciousness: "For God so loved the world that he gave His only begotten Son, that whosoever believeth in him should not perish, but have everlasting life."

I take up again the dialogue which I am trying to follow between belief and unbelief.

Unbelief says, The Gospel, as generally received, is inconceivable, and therefore impossible.

Belief answers, It is a fact, a divine fact in history, and therefore it is possible.

Unbelief replies, The testimony upon which these alleged facts are based may be untrustworthy; the witnesses may have been themselves deceived, if not deceivers. Small germs of fact may have grown and blossomed into a cloud of beautiful myths. Or, if the time of the formation of the Gospel narratives seems too short, and the date of Christ's coming too late in history for this mythical explanation, there may have been artifice and more or less conscious tendency to fabrication on the part of the early disciples.

Belief answers, The Gospels are as trustworthy as any historical narratives. But we do not rely simply upon direct and explicit testimony to the facts of the Gospel of Jesus Christ. We have other and greater reasons for our faith. These facts are necessary facts. We cannot explain the connections and course of human history, before or since Christ, unless we admit the substantial truth of the Gospels. We must admit these facts, we must accept them in their integrity; for otherwise the order and continuity of history are strangely broken. The facts of the Gospel are not what Lessing would call " accidental truths of history; " they are necessary facts—necessary to an adequate and thoroughly rational understanding of the order and issues of history. Moreover, belief proceeds to answer, These facts are not dead facts, they are living powers. The life of Julius Cæsar we receive as a matter of historical testimony, and yet, in a certain sense, it is a dead fact rather than a living one—a fact of ancient, not modern, history; but these facts of the Gospel of Jesus Christ are still living facts—living historic forces, active energies in modern history. These divine facts came into the world as impulsions from the Unseen; as powers of the world to come; and as such their strength is not abated with the years; they are still present and efficacious in modern society, in its truest life and best growth. We have, then, in the experience of Christian hearts and Christian society, under the preaching of the Gospel, the living testimony of truth to truth—the heart of man still answering to the revelation of the heart of God. The persistent vitality and continuous growth of evangelical religion are facts for which we should have some adequate explanation. Here is a marvellous fact of growth which implies throughout the energy of some hidden life. There does seem to be something in the heart of humanity which responds to the presentation of the Cross of Christ; the heart of man knows its divineness, and feels its quickening power; and, as those flowers which follow the sun through the day, follow it still though the heavens may be overspread with clouds; so, although the truth of the Gospel may often be hidden behind our imperfect interpretations of it, nevertheless, the purest intuitions, the highest aspirations, the largest hopes of humanity, do follow the glory of that true light which lighteth every man that cometh into the world. Here orthodoxy well might rest its case; here, as matter of fact, many believers do rest, contented to receive the gift of forgiveness of sin, and the love of God shed abroad in their hearts, in which they find life's best hope and sweetest joy.

But unbelief is compelled to support its reasoning against the supernatural facts of the Gospels, by bringing into question certain fundamental ideas, also, of Christianity; and so belief, too, rising from the facts of Christian experience to the ideas of Christianity, is willing to meet the appeal to reason and conscience. To reason and conscience we are asked to go; and to reason and conscience we will go. To this tribunal we would most confidently appeal; but we would appeal to reason in the highest— a reason informed with conscience, and full of heart—a reason that has power of insight into moral realities, and intuitions of the deepest spiritual truths.

The class of objections to evangelical Christianity which we have next, then, to consider, relate to the views we are supposed to hold concerning the Person and the work of Christ.

When Dr. Johnson was travelling one day in a rural district, he was asked by a country-woman how he could have defined in his dictionary a pastern as the knee of a horse. He replied, "Ignorance, madame, pure ignorance." I certainly intend no discourtesy, yet in justice to the churches I am constrained to say that ignorance of what evangelical teaching really is seems to be the occasion of not a few common objections to it. When it is said, for example, that the church founds its belief in the divine person of Christ upon the miracles which he wrought, the statement falls very far wide of the facts. It is the character of Christ which is the supreme evidence of his supernatural person. The chief argument for the divinity of Christ is his humanity. Close your eyes for the time being to all accounts of the mighty work of Jesus; seek to form a clear conception of his person and life; and that character, when once really seen, will be its own evidence, the proof of Jesus' unique oneness with the Father. Then read again the accounts of the miracles, and they will seem no longer miracles when narrated of such a Christ; they are as natural to him as our commonest deeds are to us; they are contrary to our experience of other men, but not contrary to the world's experience of Jesus Christ. The divine humanity of Christ is the citadel of evangelical faith. Miracles have still their evidential value; they are the collateral securities of faith: but why question the collaterals when the divine handwriting in the character of Christ remains unimpeached and unimpeachable?

Leaving, then, with a single word, this argument for belief in the glorious person of the

Lord Jesus Christ, which is now the ultimate and commanding reason for faith usually given by evangelical believers, I turn to another part of the objection often urged against evangelical faith in Christ.

What does the orthodox theology of to-day have to say concerning the so-called sacrificial theology—the atonement for sin effected, as the churches teach, through the sufferings of Christ? Can we be expected still to cherish a moral and rational belief in the orthodox idea of atonement?

I might, in reply, ask you to look with me through that progressive revelation of God, of which our Bible is the record and witness, and to seek, as we gaze down that divine perspective of covenant, law, and sacrifice, to determine in relation to the chief facts of the history of redemption the place of the cross upon which the Messiah died; or, I might ask you, leaving the circle of apostolic thought, to enter into the history of this doctrine, and to follow from age to age its development; and thus we should be fitted to understand those views of the atonement which are now prevalent in the evangelical churches. But I shall invite you to a shorter yet more arduous task—to attempt to climb with me straight up to the very heights. I shall urge you to endeavor to take this whole doctrine of the work of Christ up into the pure sunlight of the best and most heavenly conception we can gain of the character of God himself—the height to which this doctrine is uplifted in our text: For God so loved the world.

The first two steps along this path which I would take are indicated for me by the difficulties which are ordinarily found with the theology of the Cross. " The Bible," it is said, " teaches that the wages of sin is death. But when the church tells us that Christ's sufferings and death have substituted eternal life for this death, then our knowledge of sin—of its consequences as felt in our own souls, and as seen in others—tells us that this cannot be true." It was the first and the greatest orthodox theologian who once wrote: " Whatsoever a man soweth, that shall he also reap;" and evangelical theologians can hardly be accused of neglecting to preach, and with the utmost earnestness, the inevitable consequences of sin, and the certainty of the laws of retribution. What then? Can there be no forgiveness?

Whoever accepts the simple human truth in Jesus' parable of the prodigal son, has already risen above the course of natural retribution upon which the objector just stood, and approaches the higher ground of grace. In that parable Jesus laid down the first, broad truth which underlies the whole power and efficacy of his own atoning work. Sin, he would teach plainly, is forgivable. It is in the moral nature of God to forgive sin. The elder son might have answered, in the language of some who are troubled with our evangelical preaching: My knowledge of sin leads me to believe that sin must be punished; I see no justice in forgiving and restoring a worthless prodigal; I cannot " comprehend how any faith, of whatever nature or degree, can suspend the eternal laws" by which the Father governs the world. I cannot see how any violation of law can justly escape the inevitable penalty—"a penalty which no belief or no prayers can avert." The prodigal must suffer the " natural penalty of his sin;" " we cannot divorce one from the other." How can the Father, who governs by "unchangeable laws," make a feast for him? Are not the wages of sin death?

Over and against the elder brother's reasoning; over and against the theology of despair; over and against this hard truth of natural retribution, Jesus taught unmistakably that the Father can forgive; that in some diviner way sin is forgivable; that there is some possibility for forgiveness in the heart of the nature of things, in the bosom of the Eternal. This parable does not yield the whole of Jesus' truth; it is the beautiful beginning of the evangelical doctrine, the end of which was the teaching of Jesus in that upper chamber, when he made known to the disciples—to their afterthoughts, at least, upon his words—how, through his own sufferings, sin could be forgiven of God; how he was love's own atonement for the sin of the world.

What, then, we ask, is the divine method of forgiveness? How would Jesus reconcile for us these conflicting truths, that sin is punishable and sin is forgivable? At this point let us seek at once to take this doctrine up into the light in which Jesus left it, the light of the love

of God. I believe that the whole universe was
first for the Christ, and then Christ was for the
whole universe. I believe that the possibility of
the cross of Christ is a possibility in the moral
nature of things; and orthodoxy asserts with
grateful exultation that the Gospel of the Cross
is in accordance with our best knowledge of the
nature both of God and man, and that doubt or
denial of it dims the glory of Deity, and lowers
the dignity of human nature. Let us see if it
be not so. You remember that in speaking of
the Christian conception of God I remarked,
love is itself a trinity. I ask you now, therefore, to look up at the Cross, and to behold the
work of the Redeemer, in the light of each one
of those primal rays which form together the
perfect unity of the love of God.

First, love is benevolence—the giving of
self—self-impartation. Shall the love of God,
then, pause—shall it stop in the ascent of life,
until it has given of itself to the utmost? until
it has imparted the divine nature itself to the
heart of humanity? Love, secondly, is sympathy—the power of putting ones' self in the
place of another; and you know how human

friendship enables one sometimes to enter into the very heart of the experience of another; how human affection enables the father or mother to take the sin and shame of an erring child to their own bosoms, grieving over it, and suffering through it, as though it were their own sin and their own shame. This vicarious power of living in the lives of others is of the very essence of love—and shall God be less perfect than man? shall human friendship in its power of sympathy be more beautiful than the infinite love of the perfect God? shall the mother's heart possess a power to enter into and feel as its own the suffering and shame of a lost child, which the God who made that mother's heart himself cannot have? I say, then, that to deny the vicarious power of love is to put a limit—a limit of nature, a limit of our poor understanding—upon the perfectness of divine love, and to make God morally less than man. When will we learn, when will we have faith enough in God's own image in humanity, to dare, reverently and humbly, to look down into the depths of the purest human affections, and to find mirrored there most brightly, mirrored as nowhere else reflected from all the world beside, the very perfections of the Deity?

Love, then, in its sympathy, its vicariousness, must be able to do what its benevolence would prompt it to do in bearing our sins. But there is a third element in love—the element of right-eousness. This is love's self-respect, its true self-assertion, the affirmation of its own worth or good, eternal faithfulness to itself. This is the holiness of love; and without this element of self-respect human love would sink into license and lust. Righteousness is the genuineness of God's love. How, then—this is the very diffi-culty of the whole question—how can sin be forgivable in view of the righteousness which belongs to the very nature of love? Look again, not at any of the lower illustrations of mediation which may be derived from other all too imperfect analogies; but look at what love itself can do, at what love has done. What must it do to forgive sins against itself? If love simply should consent to take the offender back without any penitence on his part, or without feeling and showing on its part any grief and suffering for the wrong with which it had been

4

pierced, then love would indeed lose its self-respect, and be robbed of its worth and purity. Love can forgive—but it must suffer in forgiving, and by its own pain and grief for the wrong done, show its own recoil from sin, and condemnation of it, even while it forgives and delights in giving back again its trust; and there can be no genuine human forgiveness, no real reconciliation between friends, unless there be some suffering upon the part of both. Oh, my friends, perhaps this is the reason why forgiveness is for us so hard a virtue; we cannot truly forgive without some crucifixion of our very selves! We do not choose to cover the wrong done to us in our own shame and sorrow for it, and, condemning it by our own suffering for its sinfulness, to be willing and able, with a true heart, to forgive our brother; we too often would rather see the wrong condemned through his suffering the full consequence of his offence, and not by any suffering of our own for him and with him. But God in his perfect love chooses the better way of forgiveness, condemning the sin of the world, while he forgives it, through a divine sorrow for it, through Gethsemane and the

Cross! So, often, in our human homes, the mother's tears, the hairs of the father turning gray, are the signs of the sorrow through which love manifests its sense of the ill-desert of sin, its deep, unalterable abhorrence of wrong-doing, while it keeps the door open for the feet of the returning child, and is ready at any hour to take its own, lost and found again, mourned over, suffered for, and forgiven, back to its pure home and happiness. If we can do this—if we know that we can do this—if you fathers and mothers know that there is a way for human affection to forgive without dishonoring itself, though it be a way of tears—cannot God do it? Cannot God find the same way of forgiveness? Can God be less than our human hearts? But how can God suffer? How shall the infinitely Blessed One find the way of tears? How shall He condemn our sin and forgive it by suffering its wound and hurt as though it were his own? The answer of revelation, the answer of history, is the Cross of Christ. As the benevolence of God's love finds at the end and at the head of the creation the place for the God-man; as it takes the whole chain of created being up in its

last link and binds it to the throne of the
Eternal; as through its vicariousness the divine
love enters into man's very life, puts itself in
the form of man in our very stead, being
tempted as we are, making its own our experience of sin, desertion, and death; so also the
righteousness of love is satisfied—satisfied once
for all and forever—in the infinite sorrow for
sin which is manifested upon the Cross. There,
where humanity comes nearest to the heart of
God, where man approaches nearest to the life
of God, where the Deity takes humanity to
itself—there is the altar, there is the holy-place,
there is the Gethsemane of Spirit, where sin is
suffered for with an infinite and an efficacious
suffering.

The answer of orthodoxy, then, is complete.
It is an answer resting first of all upon divine
facts in history, and confirmed by the gracious
experience of Christian life. It is an answer
which is then seen to be in its ideas, also, most
consonant with our highest and best conceptions
of the possibilities of love, human and divine.
Through the sufferings of One who represents
God's whole feeling toward the sin of the

world, through love's perfect conquest of evil
upon the Cross, all the interests of the heavenly
home may be preserved, and the righteousness
of the Holy Father be manifested and main-
tained, while sinners, forgiven and welcomed,
may find free entrance into every one of the
many mansions. Should the elder brother now
say, Father, why not inflict the threatened penalty? how can you rejoice over one who went
and wasted his substance? then the answer of
eternal love is, that sin has been condemned
already; condemned more earnestly, with a
deeper condemnation, in the suffering which
has been incurred, in the very willingness to
bear with it, to receive in its own bosom sin's
deadly wound, and freely to forgive it. The
Father's sorrow expressed in the Christ, the
divine feeling of shame for sin manifested in
Christ's measureless grief for it, in one word,
divine love vicariously suffering for sin, is its
sufficient and God-like atonement. And by
that work of God in which he satisfied himself
in forgiving us, we are lifted out of the lower
courses of retribution into a higher order, into
the order of the moral universe, into the order

of moral freedom and grace. It is true we are not delivered from the purely natural consequences of sin; but does it not make a difference whether, as we suffer the inevitable natural pains of sin, we suffer them in the consciousness that they are no longer divine inflictions of penalty, since God, for Christ's sake, has forgiven us; or whether we must endure them as under the displeasure of God, in utter loneliness and banishment of spirit? Would it not make a difference to your child, who, in disobedience to your instruction has put his finger in the fire and been burned, whether it be left to suffer alone, or in the mother's arms? Does it not make a difference with us, whether, when we die, we die alone, suffering in the darkness the penalty of sin, or whether we die knowing that even in death the everlasting arms are beneath us, and that close to our fainting heart beats the heart of the eternal Love? Oh! this is what God in Christ does for us—He takes us, even while we are under many of the natural consequences of sin, up into the fellowship of His Spirit; takes us out of the dark sense of guilt, and the fear of death, up into the peace of

the Holy Ghost, and the communion of the
Father.

I have been presenting, I am aware, but one
aspect of the atoning work of Christ—that view
of it which seems to me to be the highest, most
purely ethical, and most satisfying.[4] There are
other views of it opened at different points in
the progressive revelation of God in the Bible
—other views corresponding to lower stages
and analogies of human experience. But if you
have climbed to the height of this text, God so
loved the world ; if you have once looked abroad
upon the revelations of divine things opening
like broad and luminous horizons from the ele-
vation of this truth of God, then you are above
and beyond most of the difficulties and limitations which too often narrow and confine evangelical explanations of the atonement. And here
I may safely leave it to your own better reason
—to the heart in the reason—if Jesus did not
know the very nature of God when he taught
that, notwithstanding all the appointed retribu-
tions of nature, sin is forgivable ? Unless you
are prepared to make God morally less than
man, you will gratefully own that there must

be found, as the Gospel of the Cross assures us
there has been found, for infinite love a way of
atonement—a way which even human love has
often learned through love's instinct of sym-
pathetic grief—a large, beautiful, transfiguring
forgiveness, consistent with its own pure self-
respect, and satisfying every thought of righteousness. The atonement is thus seen to be love's
perfect self-satisfaction in the forgiveness of sin,
and reconciliation of the world to God.[5]

And now I ask, in all fairness, that this teaching of the evangelical pulpit shall not be cari-
catured; that men should at least take the
pains to understand its true spirit, and to judge
it by the real morality of forgiveness. I ask
you to look at human nature on its diviner side,
and not to be satisfied with low and narrow
conceptions of its possibilities. I ask you to
admit something of the capacity of God for
loving man, and something of the capacity of
man for the indwelling of God. Man was
made for God, and God loved to give himself
to man—that is the simple deep meaning of
Jesus' Gospel. Human nature was not made
to be a little, bustling independency of God;

but to dwell in God, and God in it. I urge you to view these evangelical doctrines not simply as historical facts, but also in their ideal completeness and truth; and, when they are thus viewed, the person and work of the Lord Jesus become transcendently glorious to the reason as he is unspeakably precious to many hearts.

Let it be remembered, finally, that orthodoxy teaches there can be and is but one limit to this redeeming power of God's love in Christ, and that is the limit of a will which persistently rejects the divine. Jesus whom we love may be, as often he has been, misunderstood. Education and training, as well as the mistakes of his friends may prevent his light from shining undimmed upon many who fain would see him as his glory has shone full upon other uplifted and glowing souls; but no friend is more patient than he, or so willing to wait, if need be, through the ages for the world's perfect understanding of his work for it; and words spoken against the Son of man, he himself has told us, shall be forgiven. Evangelical theology, in remembrance of this attitude and this gracious word of the

4*

Master, would not make salvation dependent upon intellectual appreciation of its doctrines. Many a soul may grow to be Christ-like even in the dark. Christian life can spring up even around dim beliefs. A wise orthodoxy would devoutly hope that upon many souls there may dawn at the last day such revelations of light and glory from the ascended Lord, now hidden from them, as shall make their human virtues blossom into angelic beauty, and flood their lives with joy. But orthodoxy, obedient to the Master's word, teaches that there is one sin of the utmost danger, against which, with all earnestness, it would warn men again and again. To resist in aught the divine influence; to grieve the Holy Spirit; not to be willing to follow the light of God which is now manifest; not to be ready to receive and to welcome the Christ so far as he has made himself known to the conscience or the heart, that is sin, deep, dark, and dangerous—sin, which, if it grows into the habit, the determinate purpose of the life, may become the sin against the Holy Ghost which hath never forgiveness.

IV.

IMPERFECT THEORIES OF THE FUTURE LIFE.

While we look not at the things which are seen, but at the things which are not seen : for the things which are seen are temporal ; but the things which are not seen are eternal.—2 Cor. iv. 18.

TWICE during my summer ramblings I have succeeded, after a hard climb, in gaining the summit of Mt. Katahdin. I stood upon a lofty ridge of rock, on the one side of which there was a steep descent where one, had he slipped, could hardly have kept his footing; and on the other side fell a sheer precipice, partially encircling an abyss, in which the clouds boiled and surged, and the winds moaned through the vapors like the cries of lost souls.

He who once succeeds in climbing the height of evangelical truth up to which in the last sermon I tried to lead your thoughts, will be confident that he stands upon an everlasting foundation, exalted though he be above the clouds; and he will be aware, also, of the danger of losing firm foothold in the truth, or of falling headlong into abysmal unbelief, if he ventures too carelessly and too far on either side. The Biblical truth of the nature of the Godhead, if we stand upon it, will preserve us, on the one hand, from plunging into utter scepticism, and, on the other hand, from descending into untenable views of divinity, at the bottom of which lies the hopeless jungle of pagan superstitions. So the evangelical truth of the divine humanity keeps us, on the one side, from falling into sheer fatalism, and, on the other, from slipping into theories of human nature, which, though they seem at first lofty, nevertheless are sure in the end to land us in pessimism and despair. So in regard to Christian morality, one who stands upon the exalted doctrine of God's grace in Christ is protected at once from lawlessness and license, and from worldliness and merely prudential virtue—the epicureanism down which the descent is easy into lowness and vice.

But at this point I meet with another objection to evangelical religion which shall serve as the stepping-stone to our present reasoning. It is often said that evangelical theology appeals unduly to the hopes and fears of men, thereby producing a morality of mere policy. Men are urged to unite with the church in order that after death they may escape from hell. Now, so far as the objection made lies against the motives of some professed Christians, I would not care to interpose a word to break its force. Jesus himself rebuked the multitude who followed him for the sake of the loaves and fishes; and I might appeal to the echoes which linger in our churches, the echoes which linger around the best orthodox pulpits, to prove that true evangelical religion makes its appeal to the noblest motives, to whatever is childlike in childhood, to whatever is womanly in womanhood, to whatever is manly in manhood.

But, if it still be urged that any appeal to men's hopes and fears is unworthy a lofty morality, one curious fact of modern literature would of itself be enough to warrant me in calling a halt to this attack upon the church. The fact is, that this objection to Christian motives on account of what Herbert Spencer cleverly satirizes as their other-worldliness, and John Stuart Mill regards as their appeal to mere policy, has singularly enough been raised recently against Christianity by the two leading representatives of that very morality which is based upon utility, or inherited experiences, at least, of utility; while, on the other hand, Jonathan Edwards, who used to make the very souls of men tremble by his intense pictures of the agonies of the lost, was the very theologian who worked out a theory of virtue so high and so disinterested that the chief apostle of scientific utilitarianism, Mr. Spencer, who cannot even "define virtue except in terms of happiness," fails to understand it, and misstates it.

The simple truth of the matter is, that evangelical theologians are the very thinkers who have exalted most highly the idea of immutable moral distinctions, and the love of virtue for its own pure sake. Moreover, fear is a motive which is naturally and necessarily recognized in all government, in society, and even in the discipline of the home; so that those who object to the use of these motives in religion might well be left, as Bishop Butler would say, to hold their dispute with the constitution and course of nature.

The question really to be considered is not, should we be influenced by hope or fear? but, for what may we hope and of what ought we to be afraid? In order, therefore, to deal satisfactorily with the doubts and difficulties of faith which are to be met with in this direction, we should enter into a full discussion of prevalent orthodox views of the future life: What, as generally held by evangelical churches now, what, as taught by really representative minds at the present time, are the orthodox views of the future life?

Let me remind you at the outset of this inquiry that the difficulties which surround this subject, and which seem sometimes to rise up against the government of God himself—the shadows our earth in its history of sin seems to cast against the very glory of Heaven—are not the creation of Christianity. Revelation only serves to bring them out; they are difficulties which run down into the depths of the moral nature of things; they are problems which lie back in the mystery of the creation of a moral universe.

Around the second star in the sword-handle of Orion there is a remarkable nebula, which seems to hang in the skies like a bridal veil, its threads of white light woven into an infinite tracery, and through its folds stars sparkle and gleam; but this veil of light surrounds a spot in the sky of utter darkness. I have seen sensitive girls start back with a shudder from the telescope, as that veil of light flung across its field seemed to bring out, like a darkness that could be felt, the black sky within its folds. And often in the silence of the night, as I have gazed at that mystery of light and darkness in the skies, I have felt that I could form some conception of what Jesus meant when he spoke of the heavenly glory and the outer darkness. But the telescope through which I looked did not create that darkness, it only revealed it; and so the teaching of Jesus Christ only brings out the darkness which sometimes seems to be the deepest and most unutterable upon the very borders of celestial light and glory

In wrestling with this confessedly difficult

and awful subject, one of the first things for us
to endeavor to do will be to satisfy ourselves
whether we can win any conception of the future
life, particularly upon the retributive side of it,
which shall relieve our perplexities, and enable
us to bring into order and harmony all the
analogies of experience, as well as the teachings
of Scripture. I shall not weary you with a
recital or discussion of those numerous theories
of the future life which are at best only fanci-
ful; what we have to do is first to project upon
the future, so far as we can, the lines of present
experience. I shall review briefly several theories which have been suggested, not without
reason and support from analogy, and which
have found some recognition within the pale of
evangelical Christianity.

First, there is the theory of annihilation, or
conditional immortality. In one form of this
theory it is held that the impenitent, those whose
souls become in this life thoroughly wedded to
the flesh, perish at death; that immortality is
not the natural right of the soul, but that it is a
gift of God to man, made dependent upon his
obedience to the will of God, and conditioned

upon his sympathy with the character of God. Against this theory it has often and well been urged that it rests upon a literal and crass interpretation of the Scriptures; that it contra- dicts a natural right to immortality which would seem to be guaranteed by a faithful Creator in the very constitution of our nature; and that it involves an imperfect and unworthy conception of the soul to which its Maker has delegated something of his own being, and in the very creation of which He has so far limited his own omnipotence, or placed it beyond his moral power, at least, to destroy it.

I assume now the general belief in the immortality of the soul. Your hearts are the witnesses for it; your memories are the prophets of it; Christianity is the evidence of it, wrought into the very substance of history.

It is urged, then, against this hypothesis of conditional immortality that it conflicts with this natural and inalienable right of the soul to life, liberty, and the pursuit of happiness, from age to age, and through all æons—a right which would seem to have been granted by the Creator and secured in the very constitution of the soul.

There is, however, another form of this theory, which relieves somewhat the force of this argument from nature against it. It may be held that the soul does not go out of existence at once when the body dies; but that, whether good or bad, it shall continue to be through other periods of duration until it is fully ripe for its final judgment; or that all souls must be supposed to continue, somewhere and somehow, in existence until the last great day, when all probation shall be finished; and then, when this world-age shall be over, when the new heavens and the new earth shall appear, then whatsoever is like God, whatsoever bears the image of Christ, shall be presented to the joy and glory of heaven's eternal King; but that whatever is unlike God, every soul which, by a life of persistent sin, may have lost God's image and forfeited its native right to life and immortality, shall be destroyed from God's presence with an everlasting destruction.[6]

This form of the theory of annihilation apparently relieves some perplexities of the dark problem of the future of evil; but, after all, it only pushes the difficulty farther back. The real question is not, When will probation be over, when will the judgment come? but, What is to be the final issue of evil in the creation of a good God? And annihilation by a fiat of God, and as a last resort of the Creator in dealing with sin, would seem like a confession of divine inability to overcome evil with good, rather than a final solution of the problem of evil in the perfect vindication of love.

There is still another possible form of this theory, for which, as it seems to me, there might be found stronger supports from our present experience—a theory of partial and gradual annihilation. You have often noticed the power which an evil life has to dwarf and deaden the personality of a man. The process of creation was a process ever working upward —up from the dust of the earth to life; up from living matter to the human brain, the very perfection of the material creation; up along the line of human history until at the head of the creation stands the God-man in the glory of the Father. The process of love is ever upward— up from the pure child to the strong man or thoughtful woman; up to the still more angelic

grace and virtue of the spirits of the just made
perfect. But the process of sin is ever down-
ward, destroying all that is manly or womanly,
extinguishing in the lusts of the flesh the light
and glory of the soul. Our very words for
sins are derived from the natures of the lower
animals and the coarser characteristics of the
material world. As the man enslaved by his
appetites and passions sinks lower and lower,
he seems to lose soul, to lose the power of
discriminating between good and evil, and the
capacity of entering into the enjoyments of
a pure, happy home. The mark of the beast
comes out upon his very countenance; down
even beneath the level of the brute creation
does sin seem sometimes to sink the soul, even
in this present world, until—utterly hard and
coarse, a thing rather than a man—the drunk-
ard, the debauchee, the criminal, meets the hour
of his extinction. Now, suppose this course
of degradation, so painfully and so repulsively
obtruded upon us in some lives, to be carried
on indefinitely; let this process of self-extinc-
tion, of emptying the very personality, of destroying the soul, go on through ages of ages

—and what would be left at last? What but the ashes of flames? what but the graves of souls? what but the shades of immortal minds? what but a world which would be the insane asylum of the universe? Is that what Jesus meant when he spoke of him who is able to destroy both soul and body in hell?

While, then, this theory of the gradual waste of personality and loss of soul does seem to carry out certain processes of moral consumption which we can see already begun in this world, and while it is justified by some very significant analogies of our present experience of the death which is the wages of sin, nevertheless it does not comprehend within itself all the lines of our experience, and still less does it comprise all the teachings of the Bible. Opposed, therefore, to this conception, and supported by some facts and moral reasonings which it leaves out of the account, we find a second general theory with regard to the ultimate condition of the impenitent—that of a final restoration, the restitution of all things. There is certainly much in our personal feelings to give wings to this thought of the final reconciliation of all things in Christ. There are many sentiments in our hearts which leap up at the very mention of this "eternal hope." Often, through the darkness of the mystery of evil, do we not long to see shining from afar a single star of hope? And it might be urged, from the conception which we have gained of the perfect God, that He never could give up the evil, never could give up the work of redemption, until sin's last contradiction of his own glory should be turned to praise, until at the name of Jesus every knee should bow, not in fear, but to the glory of the Father. So this hope of final reconciliation of all things in Christ, dim and vague though it be, has been cherished within their sterner creed by not a few Christian hearts, and has been avowed and defended by some evangelical scholars. But comforting as this hope may seem to be, comprehensive as it is of many analogies and moral experiences, supported, also, as it appears to be, by some hints contained in expressions of the apostle Paul, nevertheless it is surrounded with difficulties; it fails to take up into itself all moral facts, and leads into fresh perplexities and doubts. There are lines of present experience which seem to run the other way, and cannot easily, even in our imaginations of the future, be bent around in the direction of this hope. There are souls now living which seem to grow less and less human, more and more Satanic, even under increasing light. There are lives which, so far as we can judge from the little arc of them to be measured upon this earth—like a parabola whose curve, if prolonged into infinity, would never return into itself— seem to recede ever farther and farther from the light and the love of God. Their direction is toward the outer darkness. Besides this painfully evident, unmistakable tendency of sin, we cannot overlook the argument for the future permanence of moral character from the analogy of the present hardness of habit. Human nature tends to become fixed in formed growths and tenacious habits; the heart seems to possess sometimes a fatal facility of hardening itself against the purest influences even of the best homes. And while there are some passages of Scripture which seem to warrant the hope of final reconciliation, if they are interpreted as literally as are the texts usually relied upon to prove the endlessness of punishment, there are other passages of Scripture which it would be difficult to bend into this theory.

What relief, then, can I find from the difficulties under which the heart bows, as under an incubus, when I think of future retribution? Is there any clear way of thought out from the perplexities which confessedly surround this subject on every side? Each theory which we have thus far tried, promises to the heart more than it can fulfil to the reason, and is found at last to lead no whither.

I turn again to the Scriptures, but I cannot find that I am able, even after every effort, to combine all their teachings and suggestions naturally, without any artifice of interpretation, into any one clear and determinate picture of the future life and its rewards and punishments. Rather I see many of these teachings as one might see the colors of a painter on his palette; they are all true colors, they all will be needed; doubtless they are complementary colors; but I do not now, at least, see them combined and harmonized as I shall hope to do when the

divine Idealist shall have finished his picture of
human history, and it shall be unveiled at last,
in that day of revelation, ready for the judgment. I cannot say that these Scriptural teachings and hints concerning the future are contra-
dictory; I cannot say that these divergent lines
of human experience shall never find a common
meeting point; I can only say that I, a mere
child of yesterday, with all the mystery of the
infinite skies above me, with this earth of
sepulchres beneath me, with this heart crying
out for the living God of love within me, yet
with this eye of reason compelled to see the
facts of sin, and penalty, and death—I cannot
reconcile all difficulties which I must feel and
learn; I do not have the knowledge by means
of which these conflicting analogies of experience may be brought to their point of stable
union, and all these teachings of the Bible be
made clear and plain.

What, then, should we do? What, as orthodox theologians who would be true to God and
to his Word, who would obey the Scriptures
and hold the Bible above creed, what are we
to think, what are we to teach?

It is first a word of humility which the ortho-dox theology of to-day should utter upon this subject—a word of lowly-mindedness which every earnest man who has wrestled with this subject will first wish to speak.

I have thus far been bringing but a negative to your consideration. I have felt it necessary to begin by proving this negative, by showing our incapacity at present to form any perfect, comprehensive theory of the future life and the final issues of evil, because we are too inclined to demand more both of conscience and revela-tion than it was ever intended that they should make known to us in this present world-age. While we should seek to be wise up to that which is written, we should not desire to be wise beyond that which is written. I want a creed covering the Bible, but not a creed over-lapping the Bible. It seems to me, therefore, that after having first satisfied ourselves that in no one theory or conception, heretical or ortho-doxistical, can we solve the mystery of evil, past, present, or to come, we need, then, to turn back and examine this whole doctrine of the future life in the same light in which our best

Christian scholarship now searches other teachings of the Scriptures; to bring to this part of
the Bible the same broad principles of interpretation which are enabling us so successfully to
find our way above many popular objections
against revealed religion, and which to many
tried minds have placed the great faiths of
Christianity above reproach and beyond contradiction.

The next thing, therefore, for us to do, will
be to seek for the purpose of revelation in its
partial disclosures and intimations of the future
life of rewards and punishments. We shall
need to mark with painstaking care, also, the
limits of revelation; and upon this whole subject, perhaps, more than upon any other, orthodoxy needs to avail itself of what might be
called the statute of limitations in theology.
We must determine, if we can, what parts of
this doctrine are purposely left in obscurity,
and what parts are brought out into the clear
light of revelation—for it is a happy and too
rare art in religious thinking to be able to locate
mysteries wisely and well;—and, then, having
located the mysteries of retribution, we may be

able, as we read the Scriptures, to gain for ourselves some very practical and urgent truths
concerning heaven and hell. That sturdy ques-
tioner, Mr. Greg, urges very pertinently that
the common theology does not so appeal to the
hopes, and so lay hold of the fears of men, as to
bring to bear a direct and powerful influence
upon the present conduct of life. What orthodoxy now should seek to accomplish, is to put
its doctrine of retribution into such a relation
to the thoughts, the studies, the pursuits, of the
men of this generation, that they shall be compelled to feel its force, and to be swayed in
their real lives by its power. But we cannot
do this simply by repeating the old words, or
reviving the reasonings of a former generation.
The very word hell has become all too inopera-
tive and inefficient—a word useful for men to
swear by; and we greatly need, as orthodox
theologians we should earnestly endeavor, to
bring to bear upon this present world, upon the
passions, the conduct, the pursuits of this life,
the power, the grand, majestic power, of the
world to come.

If men were made to realize the power of the

eternal life, as Jesus and his disciples preached it, then the great practical purpose and intent of revelation would be gained. But you will sometimes hear the sentiment expressed and applauded, as though it were a moral truth, " Give us one world at a time, and when we reach the other side of Jordan we will attend to the next world." No popular sophism could be more misleading or despicable. It is simply impossible for us to have one world at a time. Go home to your children and tell them, if you please, to have their school-days for themselves alone, without any reference to the life before them; try, if you please, to have this life in isolated sections, childhood in its place, then youth, manhood, and old age, each for itself; but do not be so foolish, so stupid, nay, do not be so impious, as to dare to go into your closet and look your Maker in the eye, and tell Him you will take the present world and do with it what you please, and by and by have the future ! The future is always in the present, and whatsoever a man soweth that shall he also reap.

But this sophism involves more than a moral impossibility. My illustration does not present the whole fallacy of it. It is also a natural as well as moral impossibility for us to have one world at a time; for, as matter of fact, in every thought that we think, in every breath which we draw, in every beating of our hearts, we are living all the while in two worlds; we are living a two-fold life—we are dwelling amid the forms of things which are seen and passing, and with the realities which are spiritual and which cannot pass away. Two worlds are ours —this world of shadows, this world of echoes, this world of strange and unsubstantial forms, which often seems to us to be the only reality; and that other, better world, unseen but not unreal, untouched but not unknown, the world of thought, the world of love, the world of the soul dwelling in the light of spiritual truth and divine reality. Take this earth out of the skies in which it lies ensphered—take the soul out of the body—take love out of the heart and thought out of the brain—if you would live in one world at a time! Orthodoxy at least does this—with unhesitating and constant voice evangelical preaching asserts this—that the future life is vitally related to the present life;

that the unseen universe holds within its larger sphere the world which is seen; that the one universe comprehends both, comprehends all— not simply the starry skies, but also the heavens in which God dwells—not merely this little earth and its visible horizons, but also that world of power, beauty, truth, and eternal rest-fulness, in which this present life, with all its joys and sorrows, all its lights and shadows, lies ensphered, as the earth is upheld quietly and powerfully in the all-encompassing sky.

But while orthodoxy asserts, thus, the immediate organic relation between this life and its future, and while evangelical preaching is burdened, therefore, with the thought of the unseen and the eternal as well as with the care for the present; a humble and earnest theology will be willing to wait for the day of revelation to make known the mysteries which still lie like shadows over its own faith. When the voice of God ceases to speak, silence becomes the only orthodoxy. Our evangelical theology would enter into the mystery and darkness of this truth in the spirit of the little child who, when asked, as the railway train swept into a

tunnel, if she were not afraid, replied, " Afraid !
No, God sees." Yes, God sees! through the
darkness, through the deep shadow of our
history of sin God sees! and evangelical faith,
while it will not deny the night-side of nature,
while it will not dispute one single awful word
of Jesus concerning the day of judgment, will
still believe in God, and wait—its heart is not
troubled, neither is it afraid. We remember
that the Master was not troubled, that Jesus was
not afraid for God, as he looked on to the end of
the world-ages; that he who spake the strongest
words of condemnation of sin which have ever
fallen upon human ears—he who possessed the
power of perfect manly indignation, but who
was, nevertheless, compassionate with a love
passing the love of woman—even when he
was enshrouded in all the darkness of our sin,
never doubted the Father's goodness; he knew
that whatever the future might be, God would
be there—God would be there in the perfectness of his beauty and his love—and where
God is, there no wrong can be done forever!
Thus Jesus Christ, whose eyes, even while dim
with tears of anguish for our sins, looked far-

5*

ther into the future than any human eyes have ever seen—who even while gathering around him the heavy folds of darkness of our sin and sorrow, for the joy set before him endured the cross, despising the shame—he, the one perfect, the true revelation of God, knew that eternity would disclose nothing which should not justify and glorify the ways of God, and show that upon the throne of the universe Love, infinite, pure, and righteous, Love that can make no mistakes, is Lord and King.

In concluding this preliminary discourse upon the orthodox doctrine of the future life, let me remind you that to our Lord and his disciples the hour of the great change for us is not the hour when the eye grows dim, and the sound of friendly voices becomes far off and unreal in death; but that hour when God comes near, and the eyes of the spiritual understanding being opened, the soul sees how beautiful God is, and how hateful sin is; that hour when the will of self is crucified, and the God-will is born in the resolutions of the new heart. Oh! that is the passing from death unto life, the great change in the history of a soul of which what

we call life and death are in Jesus' language
only the metaphors. By whatever influences
that spiritual change may be brought to pass,
suddenly as by a lightning-flash of conviction,
or gradually and beautifully as the brightening
of the dawn; through whatever processes of
experience and grace the soul may be led up to
its hour before God; the crisis of its whole age-
long history is its decision between a life growing rich unto God, or starving upon self—its
real final choice between the true, the eternal
life, or the eternal death of the heart.

V.

Whom we preach, warning every man, and teaching every man
in all wisdom ; that we may present every man perfect in Christ
Jesus.—COL. i. 28.

DISBELIEVERS in revelation seem sometimes
to suppose that if they could succeed in dethron-
ing the Bible from its place in the Christian
church, they would succeed, also, in consigning
the belief in a future life of rewards and punishments to the limbo of old and out-worn
superstitions. A friend of Voltaire once wrote
to him : "I have succeeded in getting rid of the
idea of hell." Voltaire replied, "Allow me to
congratulate you; I am very far from that." A
keen-sighted intellect, like Voltaire's, could
hardly stumble into the delusion into which
some of our lecturers against Moses and the
Bible seem to fall so readily, that if Chris-

tianity could be destroyed, we should lose from the sanctities of conscience man's natural and ineradicable belief in future retribution. Our faith in future rewards and punishments is instinctive and primary; our doubt is secondary and contrary to nature. Only when we endeavor to conceive what the future life is like, to form some intelligible ideas of what its occupations and enjoyments may be, do doubts rise unavoidably, and perplexities begin to overgrow hope, and we feel as if the faith in immortality were almost too great a truth for the human intellect to contain.

Evidently the hour has gone by for the child's picture-book of heaven and hell. Yet we may still carry God's own promise of heaven —if no longer before us as a pictured glory—at least, and possibly to better purpose, within us, in the pure affections of our own hearts. And even while we turn from all outward representations of the judgment-day, we may still keep the awe of it in our own consciences, and find the living prophecy of it in the moral separations and destinies of the men among whom we dwell.

Having already shown how difficult it is to
form any one conception of the world to come
and its issues, which shall be inclusive of all
the Scriptures, and comprehensive of all moral
truths and analogies, I have now to push the
inquiry a little farther, and perhaps to some
more positive results, in the direction indicated
toward the close of the last discourse. Let us
seek to determine the purpose of revelation in
making known to us what it has disclosed concerning the future, and in withholding what it
has left in obscurity.

Observe, then, these suggestive facts concerning the aim and method of revelation in its
teaching with regard to these matters. Notice
that the Scriptures relating to the future life
occupy but a comparatively small part of the
whole Word of God. One might print upon
fifteen or twenty pages all important texts
which throw any light upon our future existence; what we might expect would be the
major part of revelation is the minor part of
our Bible.

Observe, again, even this partial revelation
was given little by little; the doctrine of im-

mortality was gradually unfolded. In the Old Testament, trial and suffering, and the disappointment of the national hopes, were necessary in order that through the darkness the star of hope might at length break forth and shine bright and clear. And we find that Jesus began his gospel of the kingdom of heaven by putting his teaching into the forms of prevalent Jewish conceptions, gradually leading his disciples out and up into higher and purer ideas, until, just before his departure, in that upper chamber, he gave them his last and richest word, his fullest revelation, concerning the eternal life which he promised, when he prayed the Father that "they all may be one as we are one;" when he made no visible splendors, or glory of outward things, the imagery of his kingdom; but when he made human friendship, when he made perfect and divine companionship, the prophecy and assurance to his disciples of what the heavenly life shall be.

You will observe further, not only that the Biblical teaching is progressive, but also that those very disciples to whom the fullest revelations were given were most conscious that they prophesied in part, and that the heart of man cannot conceive of the glory which shall be revealed. Revelation, then, even at its highest and its best, is but in part. Revelation began with a promise and ended with a sunset; but those disciples who stood at the close of this day of the Lord, gazing into the glory of that Apocalypse, did not attempt to fix in their gospel the colors of that sunset, to portray in definite hues and determinate forms the glory which it transcends the power of human imagination to conceive.

It is very evident, therefore, that the object of revelation in these partial disclosures of the future life, could not have been to gratify human curiosity, or to answer those many questions which our hearts are always asking.

But let us look a little deeper and farther. You will observe that the Bible, in all its teaching concerning the world to come, carefully keeps within certain general limits of revelation. These limits are in part limits of nature, determined by the range of our powers in their present stage of development.

This necessary natural limitation of revelation may be illustrated by reference to a supposed process of formation of the eye, and its increasing power of vision. It is imagined by some scientists that the eye was at first in some lower organism a mere susceptibility to rays of light—some spot in the nerve-tissue becomes capable of responding to the beatings of the luminiferous waves. Now, if we should suppose an intelligence possessed of that mere germ of an eye, such a being might rightly conclude from its germinal sensations of light that there must be beyond itself some larger and wonderful sphere of existence. But, though all the colors of a sunset had been spread before it, that beginning of an eye could not have been sensitive to their resplendent hues, and the revelation of light would have found a limit in the imperfection of the eye. Suppose it, then, to have been carried to a still higher development, to have become sensitive to marked differences of color, but to be as yet without perception of distance, or depths of perspective, its apprehension of the external world not yet coordinated with the knowledge to be gained by touch and the other senses,—then there would be still at that stage of the evolution of sight corresponding limitations of the revelation of light to it.   Now, I say, that our eyes for spiritual things may be, as it were, but eyes in the germ;—from what we do feel, from the heavenly influences which do beat upon our spirits, we are warranted in assuming that there is a larger sphere of being, there is a more glorious universe still to be revealed, into whose splendors as yet we have no power to look and live; but though that unseen world may be shining all around us, revelation finds a necessary limit of its light in the present conditions and imperfections of our powers of spiritual apprehension.

Besides these natural limitations of possible revelations, there are limitations, also, of moral purpose and design.   There may be possible revelations which God might give to us even here and now, but which it might not be best for us to receive.   We have a significant illustration of the harm which might be done through overmuch revelation, in the imaginary disclosures of modern spiritualism; overmuch revelation might interfere seriously with the natural course of human life, with the regular order of those pursuits and employments which are the appointed discipline of this life, and in which, through patient continuance in them, we are to work out our powers for enlarged and happier spheres of existence; so that doubtless God has judged for us, and with a wisdom beyond ours, between a revelation adapted to our present education, practical and useful for us now, and overmuch revelation altogether beyond our present moral verification of it—a revelation whose brightness might dazzle the eye; whose very power and glory might cause the intellect to reel, and make the reason lose its self-possession, overcome by the supernal vision. Too bright, as well as too dark, a revelation might defeat the very objects of revelation. When faith shall be lost in sight the day of probation may be over. Would not the perfect vision of God be the final judgment of character?

Keeping in mind, then, these natural and moral limitations of revelation, let us now take one step farther, and seek to understand what parts of the doctrine of the future are left in obscurity, purposely left, it may be, in the shadows of revelation.

I shall mention three elements of this doctrine which, it seems to me, both reason and the Bible leave in the shadow—and in the shadow it is wisdom for our hearts to be willing for the present to leave them.

The first of these obscure elements of this doctrine is the relation of our future life to space. Space is a metaphysical idea. You may all imagine that you know what space is; but the nature of space and its relation to the thinking mind constitute one of the old, perpetually recurring, and unsolved problems of metaphysics. The Bible does not commit the fatal mistake of entrusting its truth of immortality to any human imagination of the relation of the future life to space. Suppose Jesus had attempted to make the Jews of his day understand where heaven is—to teach his disciples the particular direction and position of the place which he was to prepare for them. They possessed a knowledge of the universe too limited and beggarly to render it possible for them to have gained a conception of where heaven may be which our larger science might not now laugh to scorn; and Jesus did not try to instruct them beyond their age and capacity, but was content to tell them, " I have yet many things to say unto you, but ye cannot bear them now," "Thou shalt know hereafter." Or, suppose that inspiration had given to Moses and the prophets some such view of the future life in its relation to the present system of things as the authors of the " Unseen Universe," for example, hold to be an admissible scientific speculation, in harmony with our present knowledge of the universe ; such a revelation would have been utterly unintelligible and practically useless to the Jews of old ; and so, possibly, a revelation expressed in the terms of modern science, in twenty-five or a hundred years from now, might appear as mere guess-work to those who at that time shall have peered farther into the mysteries of creation. One added sense might open to our view worlds of heavenly felicity ; some increased development even of these poor and limited senses might enable us to answer questions before which now our wisest science must stand dumb. When you can tell me the rela-

tion of your mind to your body; when you can
locate in the brain or heart the thought which
you are now thinking; when you can locate
human affections in the body—those affections
which, though we know of no cell of matter
which is their local habitation, are nevertheless real and abiding, if anything in this world
is abiding;—then you may be warranted in
finding trouble with the Bible on account of its
silence concerning the place of heaven; then
you may require Christian theology to answer,
where is heaven; but not until you can locate
the human soul in the body, need you be dis-
turbed about the failure of the Bible to locate
heaven in the universe, or anxious about the
relation of the world to come to astronomy.

Again, the relation of the next life to time is
left in the shadow of our present ignorance.
Time, like space, is a metaphysical problem.
What we call time, indeed, is a rate of motion
to which our present vital processes have been
adapted, and to which we have become habitu-
ated. It is easy for us to conceive that this
rate may be different for different worlds;
that within the limits of the sidereal system

one day in one star, in comparison with the revolutions of other stars, may be as a thousand years. Time is accordingly a relative conception, not the same thing perhaps for the insects of a summer's day as for man in his life of three score years and ten. It changes with the more slow or more rapid pulsations of life in the animate creation; and of what absolute time or eternity may be we have no adequate conception. Eternity is an order of existence to which our present pulses of life have not been made to beat, and into which our souls while tabernacling in this mortality are not yet introduced. These words, the infinite, the eternal, are by no means meaningless to us now; they do express to us, at least, the spirit's native sense of its own birth into a higher order of existence than can be seen, or marked by the successions of outward nature. These words are not utter blanks, they are the spirit's assertion of something more than the finite and the temporal, the sense and joy of which cannot be taken from it; but these words of spiritual suggestion cannot be brought down to the definitions of the understanding, they transcend all thought. Let us not forget that the very word over which faith and despair raise so hot a contention is a word incapable of definition, and suggestive of an order of existence utterly beyond the realization of the human imagination. Part, at least, of the difficulty in the ordinary discussions of the doctrine of eternal punishment is due to our confusion of the difference between the two kinds or modes of existence indicated by the words, the temporal and the eternal, and our attempt to conceive of the one in terms of the other. But this confusion of terms is without warrant either in reason or Scripture. The Bible nowhere attempts to represent eternity by a succession of periods of time indefinitely prolonged. Scholars frequently dispute concerning the meaning of those Greek adjectives by which Jesus characterized real life and death; whether they mean endless, or for ages of ages; everlasting, or for some period of duration; forever, or as long as the object to which they are applied has its natural continuance. But it is enough for me to know that Jesus used these adjectives to impress men with

the vast, unspeakable difference between the
true life and sin in their divergent moral destinies; yet he never sought to define the meaning of these words; he left them indetermin-
ate, as they must be, to the understanding—
words of great suggestion, but not to be
measured by us in any terms of duration.
Jesus taught plainly that men are deciding
here and now between life and death, and he
used the strongest adjectives of human speech
to indicate the absolute moral difference in this
world, and in the world to come, between those
two states; but he did not endeavor to depict
before the imagination of his hearers the possible length of duration of the future life; he
did not gather together the years, and heap up
ages upon ages, in order that by a mere human
imagination of time indefinitely expanded and
prolonged he might appall them, and for aught
we know utterly mislead them as to what the
reality of the eternal existence shall be—that
final state of existence when the angel shall
proclaim that time shall be no longer. There
is absolutely no justification in Scripture for
the crude metaphysics, the vain and painful

6

fiction, of the once too customary theological massing of times and multiplication of the ages, to represent the thought of Jesus in his solemn words, tremulous with meanings beyond meanings—eternal life, eternal sin. 'I accept these words of Jesus as he uttered them, but not as they have often been misunderstood and overburdened with human definitions and vain imaginations. Jesus, as I cannot but think, purposely left this side of his doctrine in awful indefiniteness, knowing that we are not capable of receiving more than intimations of the hereafter. I accept with implicit faith these fearful sayings of our Lord, but I will not forget that he remembered our ignorance when he used them, and that his adjectives represent what to a large extent must remain the unknown quantities in the as yet unfinished problem of good and evil; and I deny, therefore, the Christian right of any theology, or any church, to trouble me with difficulties beyond the grasp of my understanding, drawn from that portion of revelation which is left in obscurity; or to disturb and confuse my faith in those truths of eternal life and eternal sin of which I can now have some comprehension, and gain some verification in my present experience, by bringing to me questions, or dark heart-devouring doubts, which may be drawn forth by a remorseless logic from the shadows of the mysteries of God's wisdom in which Jesus, with a finer human instinct as well as diviner compassion for our weakness of faith and littleness of knowledge, chose to leave them undisturbed.

Then there is a third truth which seems to be left in the shadows of the Gospel of the kingdom; and that is the nature and intent of the divine administration of Hades—the place of departed spirits—from the time the dying leave the present world until the judgment day.[7] There is a period of life after death and before that last, great day when this world-age shall be over, of which the Bible gives us some intimation, but concerning which it affords no distinct revelation. It does tell us something concerning that intermediate state; enough, at least, to assure us that it shall not prove to be a loss of consciousness, and purposeless sleep of ages for souls awaiting the great day of awakening. The parable of the rich man and Lazarus is sufficient to dispel this thought of an inter-mediate suspension of activities among the waiting dead—a supposition which would be, indeed, alike unworthy of the soul and of God's resources for its continued growth and perfect-ing. But the Bible only yields hints enough concerning God's purposes in Hades to show us how much there is still to be communicated to us, and to prevent us meanwhile from dogmatiz-ing overmuch upon this whole subject of the final destiny of the departed. There are those pas-sages which speak of Jesus' descent into Hades, and of his preaching to the dead, to a class of souls represented as being in prison; and we should interpret these passages by the same rules which govern us in the interpretation of other Scriptures. It will not do for us to take literally some text concerning the final state of the im-penitent, and then to accommodate to them these obscure passages; it would be fairer and wiser to admit that they may be intimations of some truths now missing in our doctrine of eternal punishment, and for the lack of which, if we choose to put aside utterly these hints and to forget our own ignorance, our very faith in

God's justice and mercy may suffer harm. I
will not allow myself, by any dogmatic bias, to
strain or warp the meaning of any of these
doubtful or apparently conflicting passages of
Scripture. If I cannot understand exactly what
they do mean, I can at least refrain from putting my own meanings into them. These texts,
and certain glowing passages in which St. Paul
speaks of the final completion of Christ's kingdom, do not teach explicitly a second probation,
or mean without doubt that there shall be a
final reconciliation of evil to God; they do not
alter the fact that the burden of the Scriptures
is the utter urgency of a right moral decision
now before the Cross, and they hold up no
promise of the hereafter to any man who here
and now determines himself against the Spirit
of Christ; yet so long as such expressions have
been left in the Bible, our theology ought, at
least, not to be over-confident that it has learned
the whole mind of the Spirit concerning God's
work and purpose in the interval—we know not
how long it may be—between death and the final
judgment; and these Scriptures are sufficient to
give us a needed, though too often overlooked,

intimation that the Lord has his own administration of the regions of the dead until the Messianic kingdom shall be delivered up to the
Father; and of what the Father and the Christ
are working there we need to know far more
than has been disclosed to us before we are
competent to judge the ways of God to men,
or have reason to doubt that the awards of the
last great assize shall be in accordance with
truth, justice, and mercy. I feel that I have a
moral right—a right guaranteed by these
Scriptures—to take refuge from the perplexities of the final issues of evil in my own ignorance and in the silence of God's Word; to find
peace, comfort, and hope in the merciful ob-
scurities of revelation. It is hard, indeed, for
us to imagine how the processes of life can at
any point be brought to a sudden halt; how
the mere accident of death—for death is only an
accidental circumstance, not an inward change
—can fit an untrained and unchastened Christian for the pure vision of the supernal glory.
All the analogies of experience would seem to
compel us to believe that disciplinary processes
of life must be continued after death; and in

this intermediate period, suggested by some Scriptures, room would be found for the play of those forces of moral development whose working we observe in the present life. Not, then, until the day of revelation shall disclose to our eyes the secrets of Hades, are we warranted in raising one question of our troubled understandings, or one doubt of our beating hearts, concerning the just judgments of God in eternity.

The reformers found in their day that this half-revealed truth of the intermediate life had developed into the overgrown and corrupt doctrine of purgatory—a doctrine saturated through and through with the poison of meritorious works and penance; and rightly, therefore, the reformers laid the axe at the root of the tree, and cut down the whole deadly doctrine. But back in the minds of the Christian fathers had been simpler ideas of moral purification which had grown into that corrupt Papal teaching; and back still in Scriptural ground may lie, perhaps, the germs of a better doctrine of an intermediate life, and its processes of purification and perfecting, which it may remain

for our Protestant theology more carefully to
discriminate, and to cultivate, for the healing
of many souls now bruised and wounded by
too bare and crushing dogmatism [8]. I do not
know—I speak now not for orthodoxy, I speak
only for myself—but I have often been disposed
to question as not in accordance with the truest
instincts of hearts under the illumination of the
Spirit of Christ, and as alien to an older and
better faith, traces of which are to be found in
the liturgies of the early church, that Protestant
tradition—for it is only a Protestant tradition—
which, while it permits us through all the days
of our friend's lives to bear ever upon our hearts
before God those who are near to us, and dearer
than life, forbids us, the moment after the accident of death has happened to them, to mention
before the God of the living the names which
for years have always been remembered in our
prayers [9].

So much, then, should be said of those elements of this doctrine which are left in the ob-
scurities of revelation; and when we once succeed in locating much that is mysterious, and in
determining wisely what we are not yet able to

know, or ought not to expect now to be taught of God; then, if I am not greatly mistaken, we shall find our faith happily delivered from the burden of many difficulties, which, if we try to carry them, will surely oppress our reason and bruise our hearts.

But now I wish to look at those portions of this doctrine upon which the light of revelation does seem to fall. What parts of this truth, in its whole extent too great for us, are brought down to the grasp of our reason and conscience? What lines of it can we follow and verify in our present moral experience?

The first truth of the doctrine of future retribution, which is now verifiable in part, at least, is this: God in eternity, and for eternity, shall judge every man according to his real, fully-determined character—not according to the appearance, not according to the profession, nor yet in accordance with any interrupted and incomplete determination of character—but according to the true and final reality of his being. Wherever, whenever, however, that judgment shall be pronounced, or executed, it shall be a discrimination of characters according to their

6*

inmost truth and final possibilities. This absolute moral truth of God's eternal judgments is
so firmly declared in the Scriptures, and appeals
so directly and powerfully to the moral reason,
that I will not take time in discussing the evidence of it, but will simply state it and affirm it.

Again, the Bible, as it seems to me, does turn
to the light in which our human reason. may
see this truth of the doctrine of retribution: real
and final judgment of character is a judgment
based upon, and determined by, the relation of
the heart of man to God. The decisive test of
character, beyond which there can be no other,
is the relation of the life to the living God.
This is the only comprehensive judgment of a
moral agent; all other means of judgment, all
other relations in which men may be judged,
are but partial. You cannot know fully and
finally what a man is by observing him in his
relation to his neighbor, his parents, or his
family; one man may be a good father, a faithful husband, a kind neighbor, and yet be utterly
dishonest in his business; while another man
may be strictly honorable in all his business
transactions, and yet a disgrace to the very

name of man in his home. There is no human
relation which is not partial; which encloses
manhood or womanhood on all sides, and which
can, therefore, be the means of a comprehensive judgment of character; nor can all these
relations together give the full measure of a
man. But God is all in all; and in the relation
of the soul to the God who made it, all these
human relationships are summed up and in-
cluded, and its whole life may, therefore, be
judged. If the heart be really good toward
God, it will not be bad toward any created
thing. What a man is toward his God, that he
is in his heart; that he is in the reality of his
character. Hence there shall come at the end
of time a day when God shall be seen to be
all in all, and when our whole human history
shall be brought for its last judgment under the
light of perfectly manifested divinity; when as
the souls of men shall be found in sympathy with
God, or shall be pierced by the beams of the
ineffable holiness, as they shall be drawn by a
sweet and resistless attraction to the very
throne of grace, or as they shall be repelled by
the evil magnetism of their own sinful desires

away from the One central Light and Glory, they shall find every man his own place—and it may be the mercy in the justice of God which shall suffer every man to find his own place—in the heavenly light, or in what Jesus calls the outer darkness.

There is a third and most important element of this doctrine upon which the Scripture sheds some light, and which appeals directly to our moral reason, viz.: There shall be differences of degrees in the rewards and punishments of the future life. Heaven is not one vast celestial communism. But this Scriptural and rational truth of distinctions in glory and differences of blessings hereafter seems to have fallen almost into disuse in our current Protestant theology; yet it was a church father who said that the person who denies degrees in rewards and punishments is a heretic. Evangelical preaching can ill afford, among its motives to right and beautiful lives, not to insist upon this too neglected truth, that there are, and from the very nature of virtue and moral agency there must be, differences of degrees in the happiness or unhappiness of the future life; differences of capacity, among saints and sinners, for heaven and hell. Scriptural hints should have kept us in mind of this influential truth of immediate practical concern, as it surely is, in the conduct of life. You remember we are told that the servant who knew his lord's will and prepared not himself, neither did according to his will, shall be beaten with many stripes; but he that knew not, and did commit things worthy of stripes, shall be beaten with few stripes; and in the parable of the talents we have Jesus' express declaration that unto every one that hath shall be given, but from him that hath not shall be taken away even that which he hath;—it shall be given, that is, to every one who hath, according to his capacity to receive; and he who hath not shall suffer loss according to his capacity to lose. You remember, also, that in the Sermon on the Mount the rewards which crown the different virtues are each admirably adapted to the specific nature of the several virtues; there seems to be a peculiar fitness and some law of proportion in the blessings promised. Thus the Bible does suggest quite plainly this truth, which we ought to take almost for granted, as a matter of course, without any need of revelation to teach it to us, that, as there are now differences of capacity for things good or evil developing themselves among men, and within the same church-fold, so there shall be differences of quality and degrees of happiness in the future life. In heaven every cup doubtless shall be full, but this life may determine great differences between the sizes of the cups. Each soul shall doubtless be as happy then as it can be; but what differences of capacity for love and heaven human hearts are developing now! So, then, there is a real and delightful sense in which, all along through our earthly existence, we may lay up for ourselves treasures in heaven. A man can take nothing with him from this world— the gold which he hoards up will fall into the grasp of other hands,—but what a man has gained in himself that he takes with him into the world to come;—the splendid treasures of memory, the treasures of disciplined powers, of enlarged capacities, of a pure and loving heart, all are treasures which a man may carry in him and with him into that world where neither moth nor rust doth corrupt. The eye, indeed, may lose its sight at death, and the cunning hand of the workman may lose its skill, but that enrichment of mind which may have been gained through the eye in patient and loving observation of this world, so beautiful and expressive of God's thoughts, shall not be lost, and the discipline of powers which may have been acquired through years of faithful workmanship shall continue as a spiritual capacity in the world to come. What we lay up, too, in the lives of others are riches which may return to us again in the world to come. Souls that have gone before us freighted richly with our affections, and carrying parts of our lives with them to the other shore, shall await us there to share with us once more the treasures of friendship which in them we may already have safely laid up in heaven. All that we may do or gain in the development of our powers, in enlarging the soul, in enriching the heart, in increasing our capacity to love; all that providence may gain for us through sorrow, trial, and the "withheld completions" of the present, in quickening our susceptibility of mind and heart for heaven; all these acquisitions shall enter into the happiness and rewards of the future life. Of such rewards we may well deem ourselves unworthy, and it will be of grace that we are saved; but these attainments of Christian endeavor, these rewards of faithfulness to our own powers, and our own. opportunities, are held out to us in the gospel of the kingdom of heaven as incentives to every noble ambition, every honorable pursuit, every true study of God's thoughts, and every life-long imitation of the Christ.

This, then, seems to me to be the purpose of revelation, not to gratify curiosity, but to train character; not to give the future to our knowledge, but to save our hearts for its possibilities of immortality. This mortal stage in all its lights and shadows seems arranged for scenes of probation. The intent of God in the Bible evidently is not so to open the secrets of the hereafter as to enable us to answer those questions, deep and dark, whose shadows fall upon us as we think of the past and the future; but Jesus taught his disciples to impress upon men with all earnestness the unspeakable importance for our whole future of making a right decision of life now; and to open before our aspirations such views of the future life, of its enlarged opportunities, its grand possibilities, and its divine attractiveness, as shall be to us in our toil and in our sorrows, in our studies and our business, in all our thinking, and in all our loving, an inspiration and a joy, a pure enthusiasm of spirit, and as a very baptism of grace from on high upon our daily life.

Revelation, then, to put what I would say into one word, does give to our rational belief a practical heaven and a practical hell—enough of each is declared for all practical purposes of the present life. We do know and can understand enough concerning both to lead us to put ourselves at once into training for the life of glory and virtue which we may hope through Christ to find as the heavenly fruition of earth's best life; and to fear as the loss of the soul itself, and the darkness of all true life and love, the death of eternal sin [10].

Remember, then, let me urge as the conclusion of the whole matter, that we do have Bible enough for present duty. Though the doctrines of our faith may be left in partial obscurity, and there are great spaces of shadow even in revelation, the duties of the right life are the illuminated texts of Scripture. Repent, believe, be converted, love, pray, have the spirit of Christ,—there can be little moral doubt about the nature of the life which the commandments of Christ enjoin. And though we must needs walk ofttimes in the mists, we may keep with resolute feet the way, seeing not far on either hand, yet following surely the path of duty once trod by the Master who has gone to prepare a place for us. Are we obeying that Gospel which has in its voice to our hearts the very sweetness of God's charity blended with the deep undertone of his justice? the Gospel in which heavenly mercy and hope are in harmony with infinite truth and power, as the songs of birds of the air make no discord over the deep sub-base of Niagara's ceaseless music?

VI.

SOCIAL IMMORTALITY.

And I John saw the holy city, new Jerusalem, coming down from God out of heaven, prepared as a bride adorned for her husband.— REV. xxi. 2.

SOCIETY, then, is immortal. It is the city of God which the revelator saw coming from heaven. The hope of social immortality forms the ground-tone, and runs through the whole woof of the Biblical doctrine of the future life. This idea of the immortality of society is one of those truths which might aptly be called the unconscious beliefs of the Bible. The inspired writers, almost without noticing it, or thinking about it, seem to take it for granted in all their discourse concerning the hereafter. We ought to receive with the utmost confidence those truths which pervade, like an atmosphere, the whole Bible. The everywhere understood, unconscious faiths of the Bible are the very last truths which we should doubt or question, even though it might be difficult to find in the Scriptures a single proof-text of definite teaching concerning them. The hope of social immortality—the expectation of the city of God—belongs to this order of Biblical truths. Yet so far have we departed from this all-pervasive Scriptural thought of the city of God and the immortality of society, that we sometimes hear Christians asking whether we shall recognize our friends in heaven. As though an isolated immortality were any more a future possibility than a merely individual life is a present possibility; as though God had made each soul a little drop of being by itself, and not caused every child rather to be born into the dependencies of human existence, and to come to its own life only through the lives of others. When did God ever create a single soul to abide in itself alone? to dwell unrelated and complete in the closed circle of its own little individuality? Even if we could conceive of a soul existing by itself as a solitary human atom; if it ever were possible for a human being to become a man in and of himself alone, it would be better for that man if he had never been born. An isolated, friendless life of a few years becomes almost unendurable. Loneliness prolonged to eternity would be intolerable torment. That man who can even imagine himself as enjoying heaven for himself alone is not fit for the kingdom of heaven. The perfect individual is not possible apart from society.

Very different from the severe, excessive individualism which pervades the Calvinistic philosophy of man, is the broad, healthy, social philosophy of human nature which is taken for granted in the Bible, and which gives form and shape to the revelator's vision of the coming from heaven of the city of God. Indeed, if we will but divest ourselves of merely textual and school-boy habits of interpreting the Scriptures, and seek rather to follow the movement, and to catch the spirit, and so to receive the real inspiration of the Bible, we shall find ourselves with regard to the whole doctrine of the future life, as well as in respect to many other truths, believing with a much healthier, stronger, and exultant faith. If we take pains to follow the growth of the hope of immortality through the

Bible, we shall not be at a loss to see how the whole Biblical teaching of immortality comes to fruition in this final truth of the holy city, the new Jerusalem, coming down from God out of heaven.

For the idea of the perpetuation of a chosen race, not the idea of continued personal existence, forms in the Old Testament the foundation, the broad fundamental basis, for the up-building of the hope of immortality. The Hebrews looked forward to the continuance of the family-name in Israel, and to the final splendors of a Messianic kingdom. Then, upon that broad, social ground, the hope of personal immortality might spring up, and reach its Christian perfection.

But we usually reverse the Biblical argument. We reason that the individual soul cannot cease to exist; and then, having satisfied ourselves that we personally are to keep on living after death, we begin to wonder whether we shall live also in the renewed companionship of our old friends. So we make the Biblical faith in immortality stand upon its apex instead of upon its broad social base. The Bible, we

seem to forget, rests the hope of the individual
upon the good purpose of God for the race;
the blessed life of the saved soul here and hereafter depends upon the gracious work of God
for humanity—not for the elect—but for humanity, in that Christ died for all.

When Jesus came, bringing immortality to
light, we read that he went about all Galilee
preaching the Gospel, of the kingdom. In
Jesus' speech we do not find the period put to
this sentence where our popular usage usually
stops;—we say preaching the Gospel—here it is
said, preaching the Gospel of the kingdom.
He preached not the Gospel merely of individual salvation, as though each little man were
saved for his own little self—but the Gospel of
a redeemed society, a new, purified, glorified
society, the Gospel—there is no better phrase
for it than Jesus' own word—the Gospel of the
kingdom. To preach Christ's Gospel, therefore,
is not merely to preach to you in order that you
may be saved at last, but that you may be saved
as members of the new heavenly society; not
for your own selves only, but saved in and for
the communion of the saints, and for the delight-

ful friendships and reciprocities of the society of Christ on earth and in heaven. And as Jesus preached, so he worked; and the Father was with him in that divinest of works, the creation of a new society out of the chaos of sin. This is Christianity—not a new doctrine, not another law, not a better code of ethics—but a new society of forgiven souls, founded in the love of God, and made one in the communion of the Holy Ghost.

You can hardly fail to notice how widely our common speech concerning salvation has departed from this broader and deeper Biblical teaching. I wish now to present the argument for immortality in the light of this purer and most Christian conception of the holy city of God.

We may infer that human society is immortal both from what it is and from what it is not. So far as it is now finished, and so far, also, as it is at present incomplete, human society prophesies the coming from heaven of the holy city of God.

First, then, I argue social immortality from what society already has become so far as the Creator has finished it and pronounced it good.

Let me at the outset put the reasoning before you in its bare intellectuality, and then we may feel the moral force of it through some concrete illustrations of it. Human society, then, I would say, so far at least as it is finished, is a creation possessing absolute moral worth, and therefore it must belong to the eternities. Society is not an accidental condition, a mere circumstance of human life, but a moral good in and of itself, absolutely indispensable to finite beings for their full, personal growth and perfection. The wilderness is, indeed, a necessary part of every true, great life, but in the wilderness alone no man ever reached his full stature. The least in the kingdom of heaven is greater than John the Baptist. As possessing absolute moral worth, then, and as essential to the full fruition of individual life, society is, and from its very nature must be, of the eternal. It cannot pass away.

Such is the argument for social immortality presented in the dry logic of the intellect. But, in order to realize and to keep fresh our great

7

natural faiths, in order to find the deep sources
of permanent joy, we must be guided by something better and diviner than the mere logic of
the understanding. We must search the deep
things of God with what Wordsworth calls the
"feeling intellect," the "vital soul." And surely
the vital soul entering into and making its own
the relations of human society, and the intima-
cies of pure friendship, needs no voice from
heaven to come and sing in its heart of their
immortality. Thus it is noteworthy how in
Carlyle's recollections of his father, and his
richly pathetic tribute to his wife, this native
and inexhaustible belief of the "feeling intellect" in the immortality of our lives in others,
and theirs in ours, wells up at times to the sur-
face out of the deeps of Carlyle's rugged nature.
A lesson, not without its special significance for
our age, lies before us in the contrast between
the labored and conscious unbelief of the great
mind of John Stuart Mill, who had never
known a true human childhood, who never
speaks of the touch of a mother's love upon all
the springs of his being, and whose one strong
affection ripened late upon the trunk of a life

sturdy and straight, but all too leafless and
songless; and, on the other hand, the primal
faith, greater and more vital than conscious
thought or confession, of this rugged, rustic
nature, which was full of thorns and repug-
nances, indeed, against the careless, passing
world, but which, as these "Reminiscences"
show, blossomed into at least one deeply human,
unspeakably tender, life-long love. Life-long?
Age-long rather, in itself heir of immortality!
At the close of one of these reverent memories
of his "bright one," he exclaims, as though
compelled by the very truth of the love in him
to think of immortality in the same thought
with her, "What bounty too is in heaven!"
Memory becomes itself an upward glance—the
past of love is the best prophet of its future.
"What bounty too is in heaven!" So love,
like a sunbeam, proceeding forth from the
primal source of life, can be bound by no little
earthly horizons, but, touching this world with
its brief moment of brightness, glances away, to
shine on and on in God's heavens forever.

The absolute moral worth of the society into
which we are born, and hence, in some form of

it, the eternal conservation of its good, may be known by any man or woman who will enter in a large-hearted way into any of its obligations and reciprocities. If we would believe in immortality we must live as immortals. If men are content to live as the brutes that perish, they can hardly be expected to rise to a human faith in immortality. A pure heart, expanding in the possible affections of humanity, is its own best reason for faith in immortality.

There is one human relation, in particular, which, as it may become an almost ideally perfect type of friendship, contains, to my thinking, an inexpressibly rich presage of social immortality—I mean the relation of brother and sister—a relation too often, I know, made prosaic and commonplace, but in God's thought of it, I must believe, and in some human realizations of it, ideally beautiful. When Charles Lamb might have been seen walking with the sister for whom he had willingly sacrificed the happiness of other love, upon one of those sad days when the approaching shadow of her strange visitation warned them that they must seek the only refuge earth could give until the

storm should be overpast—an insane asylum—
leading her with the straight-jacket under his
arm through the streets of London to the only
safe retreat, and waiting in his own deserted
chambers till the visitation were over, to lead
her home again; was there not in that rare
affection conquering death in life something immortal? something by its present existence
proving its right to be forever? something
which God could not have made for naught,
but which, as He looked down from his throne
among the stars upon those two friends in their
sad walk through the streets of London, in
their lifelong faithfulness of joy and sorrow,
must have seemed to his pure eye of pity to be
of great price? Brother and sister—he who
may once have been so blessed of heaven as to
have learned the real meaning of those words;
he to whom in the mystery of this life, bounded
its whole radiant circumference around by
death's darkness and the great unknown, these
words, brother, sister, may have become full of
pure depths of remembered meanings; he has
had opened in the knowledge of his own heart
one of God's own, best reasons for immortality.

Never can those sacred words, brother, sister, fall lightly from his lips; and in his inmost soul he will shrink from the debasement of those rich words in the counterfeit sentimentality of pious speech. Words to him genuine as gold, and stamped with the mintage of life's truest worth, he can ill endure to see debased, chipped, and soiled, in the small change of religious and professional intercourse; he will not accustom himself to the counterfeit use of that word, brother, in ordinary clerical intercourse and mere business correspondence; and he will wish always to retain a reverence for unselfish and radiant womanhood too sincere and holy to suffer his lips to be betrayed into the unmeaning, vulgar, cant use of that pure word—to me a bright memory of youth become a brighter hope of heaven !—sister !

But, not to wander from my theme, this relation of brother and sister, I would say, often so singularly complete and beautiful, and in its very completeness and beauty ideal type almost of a perfected society, is itself, in its own worth, a reason for its continuance after death. Its very existence contains an implied promise of immortality. It does not look as though it were made but for a moment. It must be one of the eternal counsels of God. For, if we be- believe that there is a Creator, then, I argue most confidently, a God could not have been great and good enough to think of a relationship so rich and beneficent, and then have called it forth to shine as a mere earthly iridescence, and after a moment of divine delight in it have let it go out in eternal darkness. I cannot believe that God has created such clear, steady, shining affections in man and woman as mere will-o'- the-wisps to mislead us; they are implications of immortality—they contain in themselves the Creator's intimation of their immortality. There is hardly a reason for the persistence after death of the individual mind, which is not enhanced and multiplied many-fold when we consider man as God has created him in the family; when we reflect that all of the moral motives which we may reverently imagine could have been in the thought of the Creator when he called human society into existence, are reasons which still more, and with mightier cogency of love, might lead Him to make that society to exist forever, an indestructible and immortal good.

But there is another aspect of this argument for social immortality to be taken into our view. That which is still unfinished in human society is a reason for our trust in God's purpose to complete in his own time a redeemed and perfected society. It looks, that is to say, as though the Creator had begun a good work in the formation and development of human society, which he has not yet carried to completion, and the very fact that he has begun it, and done already so much divine work upon it, is a strong presumption for the belief that he will never leave it until he shall have finished it. It would not be like God to leave his work half done. God's purpose cannot prove to be but a broken column. Every shaft must find at last its capital in the divine order of the architecture of the universe. Therefore, society, already so firmly founded and so well begun in these human relationships and affections, shall be completed in glory. This, expressed in a few words, is the great argument for social immortality which will grow upon us as we learn from experience the present incompleteness of God's own best work in human society.

To give this reasoning force and point, I need only remind you of the many unmistakable signs that human society is as yet only begun, and is very far from being finished. The best system of society possible in this world-age is only rudimentary. The outward, physical conditions of this world are fitted only for an embryonic stage of society, not for a full-winged and full-grown society. In its idea and apparent intention human society is something evidently above this earth, and for a larger than this temporal life, but it is still bound within earthly conditions. Its highest spiritual relationships are rooted and grounded in laws of physical descent. The best society is something celestial confined still within a shell of earthliness. It is useless, it is wicked to wish even to break prematurely, before death, the shell of earthly conditions and limitations within which society must be carefully matured for the free, sinless life of heaven. Human lusts breaking through the laws of the social order would quickly turn this world into a hell.

7*

Human love, growing strong and pure in obedience to the laws of the social order, makes of happy homes beginnings of heaven. Genius has sometimes felt itself free to soar above common social restrictions into an empyrean of its own; but it only repeats by its folly the old fable and melts its own wings. When did genius ever become stronger, brighter, more inspired, by disregard of common morality? Byron singed his genius in his own passion. Shelley's wild fancy might have become a steadier, higher flame, had it been fed, in one lifelong marriage, upon the pure oil of domestic truth and happiness. Goethe's poetic art was not made more deeply human and more heavenly pure by his selfish loves for women, and his imagination needed for its glorification a touch of the sacred enthusiasm of the poet who lived " As ever in my great Taskmaster's eye." Possibly George Eliot might have come nearer finding the missing truth in her life's thought of self-renunciation, had her genius not been drawn still farther into the cold shadows of the eclipse of faith in George Lewes' home.

There are, then, conditions and necessities of

human society which may at times prove
burdensome to the individual who suffers from
circumstances, or his own fateful mistakes; but
which, nevertheless, are essential to the very
existence of a growing organism of society such
as that of this earth is, and which we must
quietly accept, therefore, as for this world, at
least, the wisely ordained laws of social life.
Socialism in its various forms is a vain rebellion
against them. But if we do feel at times their
pressure upon our individuality, or if in others
they seem sometimes to be hard necessities of
toil, or sacrifice, or loneliness, we should remember that society is in the narrowness of the
bud now, not in the openness of the flower, and
some leaves may be cramped for a season before
it be full-blown. There is much in the present
system of corporate existence which is necessarily limited and temporary—much scaffolding
of the rougher elements of this world which
shall come down when the temple of God, held
in its perfectness in his eye from the beginning,
shall at last be finished. As the human body,
in which whole ages of ascending types come
forth at last completed, is, nevertheless, but the

temporary physical basis for the life of an immortal soul, and, while serviceable for the first few score years of our existence, would not do at all for the activities and possibilities of a full-grown and perfected soul; so this present form of human society is the fruition of the social instincts that have striven up to man, and answers wisely and well its purpose for a season; but it would hardly be good enough to last forever, and it shall at length give place to the higher and perfected organization of society, the new Jerusalem, the holy city coming down from God out of heaven, prepared as a bride adorned for her husband. How many present imperfections, how much incompleteness remains to be done away! Enforced separations of friends; great spaces of absence; strange interruptions of happy companionships—to say nothing of lesser breaks and flaws in the social happiness of even the best men and women; imperfect sympathies; cares treading affections down in hard, worn lives; circumstances closing opportunities; sicknesses shutting the outflow of activities; necessities and responsibilities without number repressing oft with heavy weight

the play of spirit; these, and other such limitations and incongruities of the present system of
society as we see it now begun among us, and
ourselves are parts of its imperfection, belong
all of them, as we may devoutly hope, to its
present world-and-time conditions only, not to
its eternal fruition. These earthly and temporal limitations shall fall away, as the sheath
is stripped from the ripened grain, when the
harvest shall come which is the end of the
world. The whole creation now travails in
pain together for the liberty of the sons of God.
Then, when the end shall come, when the city of
God shall be the final and perfected form of
society, these former things shall have passed
away. The physical, earthly laws of birth and
death shall have accomplished their work, and
be needed no more for the fulness and manifoldness of life in the kingdom of heaven. The
long succession of the generations shall cease,
and society become an ever-present companionship of the redeemed. The days of upbuilding
which God has carried on through the ages in
which, as Jesus said, My Father worketh hitherto and I work, shall be ended, and the day of

joyous rest shall begin. The Sabbath of society shall come at last. So Jesus thought of the perfect society, complete in the glory of the angels, when he answered the Sadducee's puzzling question concerning that poor, overmuch married woman. They could form only a low, worldly conception of what society may grow to be. They could only project the temporary conditions of life in this world into the next, as they thought of the hereafter. So they were perplexed to imagine how human society could pass on into immortality, and they thought by their shrewd difficulty to puzzle the very Christ! But with a divine insight into the abiding realities beneath passing forms of things, Jesus brushed away their vain imaginations with a single word of truth: "For in the resurrection, they neither marry, nor are given in marriage, but are as the angels of God in heaven." These familiar forms of social life are temporal; but the substance—the reality which we carry hence with us in our hearts—is eternal. The outward shall pass away, but the inward truth of love shall abide forever. For in the resurrection—when this world-age, that is, shall be over, and the fruition of all its struggle of life upwards shall appear—they shall neither marry, nor be given in marriage. Whatever in human relationships and affections was only of the earth earthy shall pass away, but love shall abide—love pure and true, radiant and change·less; for they shall be as the angels of God in heaven.

My thought has skirted but the shores and shallows of a boundless hope. The horizon of it lies ever beyond us, and as in the light of set·ting suns. But enough may have been suggest·ed to awaken in some hearts afresh the joy of this great hope. This whole argument for a com·plete and blessed social immortality rests in the last analysis upon this simplest yet profound·est of truths that God has made everything in this world and its history to grow until his own harvest time; a truth this to be found alike, in some form of it, in all scientific study of the nature of things, and hidden, also, in the very heart of Scripture. Human society is only in the germ now; hereafter shall God gather the ripe fruit of this tree of life for his heaven.

Go then to your firesides, and, as you take

your children in your arms, in the delight of their fresh lives rejoice in the hope of the immortality of the household love and joy; for of such is the kingdom of heaven. Take this blessed hope with you into the desolate home—the rooms, so empty now, where everything suggests a presence that never comes again—keep this hope singing in your heart of hearts as you still dwell for a little while amid the many fading things with which but yesterday a vanished love was clothed; there too in the deserted home, faith may hear the angel say, "He is not here, for he is risen!" Cherish this blessed truth which pervades with its sweet comfort all God's word of promise, and is near to nature's heart, that society is immortal, and the holy city shall come down from God out of heaven. Ye are come unto Mount Zion, and unto the city of the living God, the heavenly Jerusalem, and to an innumerable *company* of angels.

That bright, restful world-future we do not and need not envy, for our work may hasten the coming of that day, and by the grace of God we are the heirs of it; and the redeemed of the Lord from all the ages past wait for us, as we shall

wait also for others after us, until that day;
"that they"—as an Apostle said with a deep,
touching sense of the mutual dependence of
God's people in all the generations, and their
final completeness in the society of the finished
and perfect kingdom of God,—"that they without us should not be made perfect."

APPENDIX.

DISCOURSE I.—NOTE 1, p. 26.

This hopeful opinion with regard to present theological toleration was expressed before the recent unusual proceeding in the Free Church of Scotland had deprived Prof. Robertson Smith of his professorship. It should be remembered that the Free Church by this exceptional action has rendered no direct decision against his teaching, or the right of a clergyman within its pale to pursue critical studies of the literary history of the Bible. It cannot be too strongly urged that a real faith in God's Word can be afraid of no science. On the contrary, the prevalence of unhistorical as well as of extreme rationalistic views of the Bible, and the increasing circulation among the people of the assumptions of destructive critics who proceed from a denial of the supernatural (as in the "Bible for Learners") lay a duty upon evangelical churches of encouraging among their ministry the science of historical and Biblical criticism. Scholars of evangelical faith should be beforehand in sifting out the truth from these new studies, and in bringing the wheat from these fresh fields of investigation to the people. Protestant faith, surely, cannot be saved by any protective policy of ignorance; and any appeal in these high matters to popular prejudice or ecclesiastical fears is unworthy the Protestant Church. Should a conflict similar to that now going on in the Free Church of Scotland ever arise in our own land, it is devoutly to be hoped that impossible, because utterly unhistorical, theories of inspiration may not betray any church into the suicidal policy of laying hands of ecclesiastical violence upon the sincere and candid Biblical scholarship which in its own better way finds the authority and power of God in the Scriptures. The beginnings of intolerance toward more scientific views of revelation and inspiration should be discouraged everywhere by all good men who believe that the Word of God is able to stand in its own commanding truth, and that it does not need to be propped up by any mechanical devices of human invention. Free and thoughtful discussions, not ecclesiastical bulls, are what the interests of faith and the truth of God's Word demand of theological leaders at the present time.

DISCOURSE II.—NOTE 2, p. 50.

I do not forget that not a few sentiments of humanity and fraternity may be gathered from classic writers, particularly from the later Stoics, such as Mr. Lecky in his "History of European Morals" has taken pains to collect; the darker side, however, of the history of the decaying empires of the Old World makes itself painfully felt. Neander in one of his minor, and I believe untranslated writings ("Wissenschaftliche Abhandlungen," s. 140 f.), with his usual profound historical analysis, has probed to the quick the moral incompetency of the ancient social philosophy. The pre-Christian ethics were powerless to create, and even to conceive of, the one true society, the real brotherhood of man. In this essay on the "Relation of Hellenic to Christian Ethics," Neander quotes the remarkable saying of Zeno, that there shall be one life and one world, as one flock led by a common law; but he shows that antiquity possessed no power to realize this conception, and that the idea itself, moreover, was defective and unrealizable. It resembles an unclear, communistic idea of society, a tendency to reduce humanity to an inorganic mass, ending in the dissolution rather than the fulfilling of the natural differences and original orderings of society (Ibid., p. 152). Neander concludes this comprehensive survey of the ethical course of antiquity with these weighty words upon Neoplatonism: "So we see the development of ancient ethics, in opposition to the principle of a divine humanity to be realized in all, which has been brought by Christ into the world, close with that egotistic, aristocratic, particularism." (Ibid., p. 214).

For a full substantiation of the statement made above, I need only refer, among recent books, to Uhlhorn's " Conflict of Christianity and Heathenism."

DISCOURSE II.—NOTE 3, p. 56.

From an exalted ethical conception of the Divine Reality, large and illumined views open out in every direction through our theology. To gain it is therefore the first duty of the Biblical theologian; and if theology is surveyed from any lower point of view, all the doctrines will be thrown out of their true relations and right adjustment. Frequent points of confusion and contradiction in our doctrinal lines indicate that we have started them from some too low, partial, or unmoral idea of God. Could we gain a perfect moral apprehension of God, such as the sinless Christ possessed, all doubt and perplexity would disappear from our thought of His ways and works.

The ethical, rather than the metaphysical, being of God, it should ever be remembered, is the subject of revelation, as the Bible is the book of religion rather than a system of philosophy. A real knowledge of the true God can be gained only through a true life, as Jesus (Jn. xvii. 3.) identifies knowledge of the only true God and eternal life. So, also, 1st Jn. v. 20.

The philosophical advantages of an ethical method of apprehending the idea of God are such as these; viz., 1. It lifts thought out of merely metaphysical difficulties and subtleties. God as love is a positively known God, however finite and inadequate may be our thought of him. Christian theology does not have to do with a blank Absolute, or negative Infinite, or metaphysical Indifference, but with the living God, the Father of spirits, who has revealed himself in his essential reality as love. 2. It overcomes deism while it saves the truth at the heart of pantheism. The ethical conception of God is the reconciliation both of the immanence and the transcendence of God. God as the supreme Moral Power must be both above and in his creation. His relation to the created universe is primarily ethical; and the physical and metaphysical nature of things, and their relation to the divine Will, are to be studied and interpreted in Christian theology under this higher and primary ethical relation of the Creator to his works. Love is at the heart of things, as it is the essential nature of God. 3. From this ethical method we gain a consistent conception of God's unchangeableness in relation to a changing world. Immutability is a moral predicate of God. He is a constant providence, a continuous thoughtfulness, over us and through history. Historical sameness in the divine conduct of the world might be moral mutability. On this subject especially see Dorner, "Christliche Glaubenslehre." 4. This ethical conception of the nature of God is indispensable to any Biblical view of the person and work of Christ (as shown in the third discourse). 5. In the light of the moral revelation of the divine glory we can read most intelligibly the Scriptural intimations of the triune nature of the Godhead. The words used in the Bible, the Father, the Son, imply real distinctions, an ontological Trinity; but the revelation of the unity of the Father and the Son, which is vouchsafed in the Bible, presents it predominantly in an ethical light for our present thought of it. God as love is blessed forever in the communion of his own triune Being. God is not revealed to us as a blank unit, but as a living unity, possessing divine society in himself, and morally and spiritually complete in his own manifoldness of being. The creation, thus, is in no sense necessary to the perfectness of the triune God over all blessed forever. Thus, as a relation in love, Jesus, "the Son of his love," speaks of his own oneness with the Father. Jn. xvii. 21, 24. The doctrine of the Trinity is more accessible to our approach from this moral apprehension of it than it is from the metaphysical side. We are obliged, however, to distinguish in thought what may be one and inseparable in God and the nature of things; viz., the moral and the real, the reasonable and the actual, the ethical and the ontological. It is one of the profoundest ideas of modern German thought that "the ethical has in it, also, something ontological.

DISCOURSE III.—NOTE 4, p. 79.

The following note is designed to indicate more fully the relations of the view of the atonement given above to other theories of it, and also to suggest certain directions in which it may be profitably thought out.

The form of our conception of Christ's work depends ultimately upon our idea of God. If the divine Will be made the one-sided centre of theology, as is frequently the case in Calvinistic discussions, then the whole conception of the atonement will be thrown out of moral adjustment, and at more than one point it will cause friction with the moral sentiments. The centre and radiating point of our reasonings concerning redemption should be a thoroughly spiritual and ethical belief in God as love in its comprehensive integrity. Starting from this idea of God, and recognizing God's eternal will of reconciliation as grounded in his ethical perfectness as love, we have then to view the incarnation and atoning work of Christ as the necessary outgoing and satisfaction of God's own moral being in forgiving sinners; and then to contemplate the fact of Redemption in its various historical relations to law,

8

sacrifice, moral government, and the power of sin.
We need not reject utterly other partial views, and
lower analogies which may serve to illustrate different
aspects of redemption; but from our higher ethical
conception we should work down among these imperfect
views, and along these lower lines, correcting what is not
purely spiritual in them, and bringing their partial truths
into harmony with the central idea of love.   The relations of law, government, honor, covenant, public justice,
etc., express real relations of the highest personal Love
to the universe; and theories of atonement based upon
them (as the chivalric, or Anselm's, the governmental,
the juridical, the federal, etc.) correspond, each and
all, to something true in God or man; but they rest
upon partial and secondary truths, and should be recognized and used as derivative and secondary conceptions of the original and comprehensive truth that God
so loved the world that he gave his only begotten Son.
The personal (ethical) relation of God to man is before
the governmental; it is first in the order of time and of
thought; and, above all dispensations of covenant and
law, it remains the primary and supreme relation of
man to the Father of spirits.   Before the law was
given, Adam was born a living soul, and man is first
and in his essential moral being a son of God.   The
vicarious work of the second Adam satisfies and can
harmonize all other necessities, all historic relations of
God to the world, because it is the completion and per-

fect moral satisfaction of this first, personal relation of the Father to the son that was lost and is found.

The necessity of the atonement, according to this view of it, lies in the moral fact that God is not, and as perfect Love cannot be, eternally reconciled to sin in himself, in the quiet depths of his own pure being, without some activity of righteous Love in view of sin;—reconciliation is not a mere state, if one may so speak, of the divine consciousness, but it is the act of an outgoing God toward the sinner. It will be seen, therefore, that our idea of the atonement, though starting from a supreme moral thought of God, is not a merely subjective view of it. Sin has become objective in a history of wrong-doing—objective, too, both as the fact of guilt, and as the power of evil in the world. But, beginning as we do with the purely moral, primary personal relation of God to man, we can then hope to survey in their true light, from this centre and height, the various historical relations and transactions of God toward man, and of man toward God, such as law, revelation, promise, disobedience, sin, penitence, rejection of the Holy Spirit.

The view of the Atonement which I have suggested, may readily be worked out critically in reference to prevalent theories of it. Thus, the older juridical and penal theories begin with a genuine idea of righteousness, and the demands of strict justice, but they fail to recognize with clear ethical insight the essential oneness

of all moral predicates in the divine nature, and hence
their necessary unity in all revelation or activity of
God in history; and they proceed, accordingly, to conceive of the nature of Christ's work too much under
the domination of some one divine attribute, or in view
of the demands of some special moral relation of God
to the universe, making the requirements of justice, or
law, or the divine veracity, or the terms of a supposed
covenant, their rule and measuring-rod for the work of
perfect Love in forgiving sin; and hence these theories
run into legalism, or artificial imputation, or even into
a quantitative substitution of Christ's suffering for the
penalty of sin; and they fail in proportion to be understood by the simple Christian conscience, or to carry
the full consent of Christian hearts.

On the other hand, the New England, or governmental theory of the Atonement, reacting from these
artificialities of the older theology, begins with certain
well defined moral axioms rather than from a deep
ethical consciousness of grace; and it proceeds by a
dialectic method rather than through spiritual insight,
to analyze the nature of the Godhead into different
species of benevolence and justice, and to construct a
series of moral plausibilities concerning the divine
government of the world, and the purposes secured
under it by the sufferings of Christ, which are logically
connected and satisfactory to any one who does not
venture to question its definitions, or whose spiritual

thirst for reality in theology does not lead him beyond its phraseology to search for the fountains of moral truth and spiritual life. As the governmental theory does not begin far enough back, so it does not end in the comprehension and fullness of all other theories of Atonement, as we may be sure the true and final philosophy of it will do; but we find that it divides farther down into two different modes of thought, one the moral influence theory, the other a tendency to return toward older theories in the feeling that some deeper, spiritual truth of Christ has been lost. The governmental theory, unless we take its truth up into some larger spiritual thought of God, is in danger of leaving for us a reconciliation of policy, rather than from the heart of God.

A few words may need to be added to prevent misunderstanding of the view of the necessity of suffering in forgiveness which has been outlined merely in the sermon upon this subject. 1. With regard to the person of Christ, and his qualification for the work of reconciliation, it should be noticed that both natures, and their union in Him, are as necessary upon this view as in any other theory of his atoning sufferings. Both the vicarious principle of love in God, and the capacity in human nature for vicarious representation, are met in the person of Christ; so that in his sufferings for sin there may be the perfect recognition on the part of humanity of the righteousness of love which cannot forgive without at the same time condemning sin in sorrow for it, as well as the perfect outgoing and manifestation on the part of God of his *whole* feeling toward sin in Christ upon the cross.

The person of Christ is seen to be necessary in still another light, when we ask the question, why could not God's eternal will of forgiveness through suffering have been carried out without the incarnation and death of Christ? Why could not the Father, taking the sin of the world to his own heart, out of his own pure divineness have forgiven it? We have seen that the righteousness of love is a moral necessity of suffering for sin in forgiving it. But the perfectness of God's being precludes the thought of God's suffering in Himself; He cannot be conceived as suffering in his own pure divineness, but only in some outgoing from himself, in some vicarious entering into the life of the world, and its sin and shame. The Incarnation, which independently of sin we hold to be the consummation of creative love, becomes in view of sin the possible mode of God's participation in the shame and the pain of our human history. God in Himself is God over all blessed forever; God going out of Himself in the form of man becomes the suffering Godman. There is an intimation of this twofold truth, of this divine unity of blessedness and sorrow, even in vicarious human suffering; for there is with those Christlike ones who suffer for the sins of others a double consciousness—a heart at peace in God, secure and restful in its own gracious goodness, beneath the sympathy and behind the suffering of the heart going forth in compassion and tears for others. Indeed, this deeper consciousness of good, this reserved power of blessedness, is necessary to genuine vicarious suffering for others; our sympathy never would be unselfish and life-giving to others, were there not this higher consciousness of love, restful in its own felicity, behind it. So the blessedness of the eternal Father is the peace and security of Heaven above the darkness and the passion of the Cross!

The sufferings of Christ, I hold, therefore, are not merely modes of manifestation of God's feeling toward sin—an exhibition on earth of "a superhistorical process in God himself." For "the reality of reconciliation" they are necessary. The incarnation is the necessary and real form of divine suffering for sin. In union with man, in the one Person of the Godman, the efficacious suffering of Love for sin is both possible and actual. Christ's passion is thus more than a manifestation, it is a realization of the love of God in immediate, organic relation to man's life of sin in the world. Our statements will thus be seen to avoid entirely the old error of patripassionism.

In this view of the atonement the extent of it is determined, not by any arbitrary election, or secret will of God, but by God's eternal will of redemption, which is grounded in his essential nature of Love, and realized in Christ's assumption of the very nature of man. Its extent can be limited, then, only by the breadth and height of God's love on the one hand, and the last and lowest limit, on the other hand, of the nature which the Son of man assumed. Any other limitation would make Christ cease to be the representative and head of our race, and would contradict our idea of God.

One more remark is in point. A distinguishing merit of this endeavor to conceive of the work of Christ in its primary and supreme relation to Love, seems to me to be the circumstance that it enhances our sense of the higher naturalness of Christ's life and sufferings. They were not imposed, that is, by mere Will, by an arbitrary decree; they were not invented by divine Wisdom as an after-thought of mercy for the propitiation of justice. They grew spontaneously, as it were, out of the very nature of God, and came to Christ in the natural working out of his mission from the Father. This higher moral naturalness both of the unique Person and the unique work of the Christ, is one of the most fruitful and grandest conceptions of modern theology.

DISCOURSE III.—NOTE 5, p. 80.

It did not come within the original plan of these discourses to follow out this view of the Gospel of forgiveness in its relation to morality and influence upon character. Justification, or love's free welcome of the sinner through Christ, is the first condition of a new, quickened moral life. Orthodox theology has much that is fresh and inspiriting to say of the creative power of manhood which proceeds from the Christ. The source and life of morality is contained in the truth which St. John felt,—We love him because he first loved us. God is before us in our own virtue, and in the growth of character, as He is before us in our thought of him, and in all our life. True morality is applied religion, and there can be no human goodness without something from God in it. Evangelical faith secures, thus, and vitalizes every moral instinct. But the consideration of this fruitful subject would itself require a volume.

DISCOURSE IV.—NOTE 6, p. 91.

Among those who advocate the possibility of conversion after death and before the last judgment, Rothe is careful to insist that "even at best the result of conversion in the kingdom of the dead . . . . would remain far behind the perfected condition of those who during this life in the senses, and not first, indeed, upon the death-bed, have turned themselves to the Redeemer." ("Theo. Ethik," § 796). This conclusion Rothe reaches from his view of the relation of the

8*

spirit, as a transforming and appropriating power, toward outward nature; he holds that, relatively, the earlier the conversion, the richer the fullness of spiritual life that may ensue.

DISCOURSE V.—NOTE 7, p. 123.

The Westminster Confession says : " The souls of the righteous, being then (immediately after death) made perfect in holiness, are received into the highest heavens, ... and the souls of the wicked are cast into Hell . . . . Besides these two places for souls separated from their bodies, the Scripture acknowledgeth none." (Chap. xxiii.) But, as the same Confession places above itself the Word of God, it may be deemed permissible to quote against this positive declaration the following Scriptures : Job xxxviii. 17. Gen. xxxvii. 35, xlii. 38, xliv. 29, 31. Ps. xvi. 9, 10, xviii. 5, xlix. 15, lxxxviii. 12, lxxxix. 48, lxiii. 9. Ez. xxxii. 17–32. (See Oehler, " Theo. d. A. T.," 1, § 259. Also art. " Hades " in " Herzog's Encyclop.") Beside these texts from the Old Testament should be placed the passages from the New Testament given in the following note. It should be remembered that according to the New Testament the souls of Dives, Lazarus, and Jesus, after death are represented as going to Hades.

DISCOURSE V.—NOTE 8, p. 128.

The Biblical elements of this doctrine may be briefly summarized as follows :

I. Those words of Jesus which refer to a time or state of existence between death and the last judgment; viz., the promise to the thief upon the cross, Luke xxiii. 43 ; and the parable of the rich man and Lazarus, Luke xvi. 19–31. Jesus used a word which the thief, with his Jewish ideas, could understand, Paradise. The promise implied that the crucified Messiah would be at once after death present, recognized, and influential among the departed. It is thus an anticipation of the Apostolic teaching of the descent into Hades, 1st Peter iii. 18–19. The second passage cited (the parable of Lazarus) contains the following truths : 1. A retributive state begins after death. Each character of the parable begins in Hades to receive according to his moral capacity and deserts. 2. The dead are not yet finally separated and judged. They exist each in his own place and manner in the same world of the dead. There is conversation between Abraham and the rich man. 3. The good can do nothing to change the condition of the bad. The bad can do nothing to hurt the good. Beside all this (or, " In all these things ") there is a great gulf fixed between them ; for good or evil they cannot go to one another. Now is our time for Christian influence, for " the night cometh, when no man can work." 4. Nothing is taught clearly concerning the effects of his torments upon Dives, and Jesus lets the curtain fall over his final state. The parable leaves him in suffering without possibility of help from Lazarus or Abraham. It does not come within the scope of the lesson which Jesus was intent upon impressing, to give any information as to whether or not a better mind might begin to be wrought in Dives through his punitive sufferings, or whether the gulf, impassable to human pity, could ever be crossed by the divine mercy. The parable teaches directly nothing at all upon these points, and would not be inconsistent with any revelation which might be made concerning the last judgment. We must take the parable for the obvious truths which are its first intention. 5. It teaches that character may become so determined at a lower stage of revelation as to render it morally certain that it would not change under a higher revelation (v. 31).

II. The apostolic teaching of the descent into Hades. 1st Peter, iii. 18–22, iv. 6. The weight of modern interpretation is on the side of taking these words to mean exactly what they seem to say. The traditional orthodox interpretation either leaves them unexplained, or refers them allegorically to the deepest sufferings in spirit of the Messiah, or resorts to various artificialities of treatment; as Calvin regards Christ's preaching to the spirits in prison as addressed to the souls of the pious dead of the Old Testament, and coolly justifies his grammatical liberty with the text by saying that the apostles often substituted one case for another! This passage, if taken to mean what the words say, yields the following teaching: 1. Christ really went to the place of departed spirits. 2. He went in his quickened spiritual life to the dead. The expression, quickened, or made alive in spirit, refers here as elsewhere to the life of the resurrection. In that form or mode of being in which after death he was made alive in the spirit, Christ went and preached to a class, at least, of the dead. 3. This advent of the crucified Christ in Hades was not a still deeper humiliation, but the first moment of his exaltation, the beginning of the glory of the resurrection. It was the Lord who had conquered death, and had begun to be made alive according to the power of the resurrection, who appeared in Hades. It is noticeable that in the mind of the Apostle the going to preach to the spirits in prison is directly associated with the resurrection, and ascent into heaven (v. 22), as though these were all parts of one and the same quickened life. The hour of Christ's advent among the dead is not determined by the text; the general opinion has been that it took place before the resurrection (so Alford, in loco); but the older Lutheran theologians placed it " after his quickening in the time between that and his going forth from the tomb" (Huther, in "Meyer's Com." in loco). It evidently was before the *manifested* resurrection on the morning of the third day; but the implication of the text is that it was after the quickening, or actual beginning of the resurrection. Our conception of it at this point will be determined by our general view of the resurrection. If we conceive of the resurrection as a supernatural development of life, a process of glorification, not a catastrophic change, then this Scripture, together with others, would indicate three chief epochs in the resurrection of Christ; viz., his presence and working among the departed in the beginning of the new life made after the spirit; his appearance on earth to the disciples in a body, in which his personal identity was recognizable, but which as possessed of higher powers was by no means the " self-same body " which died—the period of " *manifested* " resurrection; and, finally, the vanishing into invisibility, the conclusion and perfecting of the resurrection in the ascension and glorification of the Lord. The spirits in prison may be, accordingly, in the beginning or first era of the resurrection-life, having the pledge of its final completion in the glorified humanity of Him who is the first fruits of the resurrection. 4. Christ in the first moments of his quickened life went to Hades to preach the Gospel. Any other interpretation of this word, as the idea that it was a preaching of condemnation, is, as Huther remarks, " a wholly arbitrary supposition." As the rising Redeemer and Lord, Christ entered the region of departed spirits. In the fresh, opening power of the resurrection and the life he preached to the dead. To imagine that he went there in the new-born joy of his triumph over death to tantalize hopeless spirits by announcing glad tidings which could do them no good, would be to deny the very spirit of Christ, and to contradict the love of God which he had just shown upon the cross. 5. We rightly infer that this preaching the Gospel among the dead by the rising Lord, was the completion of his prophetic office, being necessary to the universality of his gospel, and the absoluteness of his work of redemption. 6. The mention of a particular class of the dead may have been suggested by the figure of baptism in the context; but these departed spirits certainly could not have been selected by Christ to receive his message on account of any pre-eminence in piety or faith. On the contrary, it appears that they were spirits of men who had lived in one of the worst ages of human history; that they had been disobedient, or unbelievers; and the expression "in prison" would seem to indicate that they were not in paradise, or partakers of the freest spiritual life of Hades. Inferences from obscure Scriptures should be put forward with great hesitancy; but if any inference be permissible from these circumstances, instead of saying with Calvin that these were spirits of the "pious dead," we should be warranted rather in surmising that they represented the lowest and most sunken of the dead before Christ's coming ; and that as he sent his disciples into the high-ways and hedges to invite the blind and lame to the wedding-supper of the Lamb, so he descended himself to the very bottom of Hades with his gospel. Thus the universality of his preaching would enable him to become at last the judge both of the quick and the dead. From 1st Peter iv. 6, Huther (in Meyer) con-cludes that by the dead are there meant "all whom Christ at his coming shall find as dead." "It is said that to all—irrespective of when or how—who are dead at the time of the judgment, the Gospel shall have been preached." 7. Nothing is said or implied concern-ing the effect of Christ's preaching among the dead.

III. To these passages relative to the intermediate life should be added those expressions which indicate that the Apostles looked forward, not so much to the hour of death, as to the last great day, the final coming of Christ, for the end and confirmation of their faith. Phil. i. 6. 1st Peter v. 4. 2d Tim. i. 12, iv. 8. 1st Thes. iv. 13–17. Col. iii. 4. 1st John iii. 2.

IV. Besides these direct teachings and suggestions of the New Testament, there are other passages which throw indirect light upon this subject, or themselves receive light from the Scriptures already considered: *e.g.*, Rev. vi. 9–11 ; Jn. xiv. 3—an intimation that the risen Lord will still have a work of preparation to do for his disciples. Mark xvi. 15, 16 ; 1st Tim. ii. 4–6 ; Luke xix. 10 ; 1st John ii. 2—assertions of the universality of the preaching of the Gospel. Luke vii. 11–15—prolongation upon earth of probation after death had ensued, which could not be if at death the final judgment takes place. Matt. 12. 32—implication, perhaps, of forgiveness for other sins than that against the Holy Ghost in the world to come. 1st Cor. xv. 29; Rev. xx. 13–14.

Such are the Biblical elements of the doctrine of the intermediate life, and they ought not to be quietly ignored by orthodox theology, or left unadjusted to our whole teaching concerning the last things. If it be said that there is danger that the consideration of these obscure passages might lead individuals to whom the Gospel is now preached to cherish fallacious hopes of a second probation after death, it is also true that the failure to take into account these hints and possibilities of Scripture may involve for us the righteousness of the government of God in great difficulty, and betray us into an un-Scriptural dogmatism with regard to God's dealing with those who die without the Gospel. The only really dangerous thing is error—to go beyond, or to fall short of, the truth of revelation. Romanism in Luther's day had gone far beyond it; but that is no reason why Protestantism should now fall short of it.

This whole subject of the intermediate life, as was intimated above (p. 182), needs further to be thought out in connection with improved modern conceptions of the resurrection. If we regard the resurrection as a process of spiritual embodiment, beginning at the death of the individual, but dependent for its full completion and manifestation upon the conclusion of this whole world-economy; then it will be easier to harmonize in one consistent idea those Scriptures which imply that the resurrection is "a present and continuous reality," wrought through Christ's present power, and those passages in which it is regarded as a still future event. The successive epochs in Christ's rising from the dead into the glory of the heavens become thus typical and light-giving. It is a possible suggestion that, as Jesus' resurrection was manifested for our sakes (visibility not being a constant, or necessary part of it), so the first resurrection, Rev. xx. 5, may be likewise some exceptional manifestation of the power of the resurrection in the appearance of saints fitted and chosen for some special ministery, who, nevertheless, must wait with all the dead, both the great and small (Ibid., 11–12), for the last great day to attain in the new heavens and the new earth their full and final perfection.

I have elsewhere indicated my views upon the process of the resurrection ("Old Faiths in New Light," chap. viii.); but while a discussion of the better form in which this blessed hope may be conceived did not fall within the immediate scope of these sermons, I would call attention here to the importance of considering it in close connection with the doctrine of the intermediate life. This seems to me to be the missing link in Dr. Whiton's recent book upon the "Gospel of the Resurrection." While bringing out forcibly the Scriptural testimony to a present and continuous resurrection, Dr. Whiton seems to me to fail to grasp the full doctrine of the Bible, because he misses this idea of a resurrection begun, indeed, at death, and begun according to spiritual law, but dependent for its completion upon the connection of the individual with the whole creation and its glorification in Christ. (Rom. viii. 19–23.) The individual neither in this world, nor the world to come, can be made perfect alone. The fruition of the hope of the resurrection-life is conditioned upon the consummation of all things. The resurrection is not merely a development according to the spirit from within, as Dr. Whiton rightly holds, but also a development conditioned upon great cosmic forces. (See Dorner, Opus cit., § 958.)

This idea would relieve Dr. Whiton's argument of no little strain in the exegesis of those Scriptures which lead hope forward to the second coming of Christ, or final form of His presence, and the regeneration of all things. It should never be forgotten that in the Biblical philosophy of salvation the life of the individual is bound up with the life of the whole, and reaches its fulness and completion only in the liberty for which the whole creation waits.

DISCOURSE V.—NOTE 9, p. 128.

The belief of the primitive Church respecting prayers
for the dead has recently been collated and carefully-
examined by Canon Luckock in his book, "After
Death." "The conclusion," he writes, "from a full
consideration of the foregoing arguments is, that the
practice of praying for the faithful dead was universally
adopted in primitive times; and though, as we have
seen, for wise reasons it was allowed to drop almost
entirely out of our public worship, yet such a state of
things cannot possibly be regarded as permanent" (p.
252). Referring to the mediæval abuse of this primitive custom which led to its abandonment in the Reformation, he says: "We may well believe that in the
temporary obscuration of the primitive practice, and
the almost complete withdrawal of what is confessedly
a most consolatory doctrine, we can see a distinct sign
of a punitive purpose, and a visitation upon this and
preceding generations for other men's sins" (p. 245).
It is certainly a fair question whether in a deep consciousness of the oneness of Christ's kingdom in this
world and the world to come, we might not now safely
avail ourselves in public worship, as well as in private
devotion, of such expressions with regard to the dead
as are to be found' in the epitaphs in the Catacombs,
and in the ancient liturgies of the church. So St. Paul

expressed out of a full heart his wish that the Lord might grant to Onesiphorus to find mercy in that day. 2d Tim. i. 18.

DISCOURSE V.—NOTE 10, p. 137.

While I have not cared to burden these pages with citations from the extensive modern literature upon these subjects, I would acknowledge my sense of the great value of Prof. Dorner's grand contribution to theology in his "Glaubenslehre," the last volume of which, containing his discussion of eschatology, has come to hand since these discourses were prepared. He puts forward the element of freedom as the reason for dogmatic uncertainty in our judgment of the final state of all men (2d Bd. §. 968). His whole discussion of these themes I would commend to the attention of theologians of our own churches as an example of the calm, catholic tone and temper which is greatly needed in the consideration of these difficult questions upon which Revelation is fragmentary, and where too confident judgment may easily betray us into untruthfulness to the heart of faith.

Old Faiths in New Light

BY

NEWMAN SMYTH,

Author of " The Religious Feeling."

One Volume, 12mo, cloth,   -   -   - $1.50.

This work aims to meet a growing need by gathering materials of faith which have been quarried by many specialists in their own departments of Biblical study and scientific research, and by endeavoring to put these results of recent scholarship together according to one leading idea in a modern construction of old faith. Mr. Smyth's book is remarkable no less for its learning and wide acquaintance with prevailing modes of thought, than for its fairness and judicial spirit.

CRITICAL NOTICES.

"The author is logical and therefore clear. He also is master of a singularly attractive literary style. Few writers, whose books come under our eye, succeed in treating metaphysical and philosophical themes in a manner at once so forcible and so interesting. We speak strongly about this book, because we think it exceptionally valuable. It is just such a book as ought to be in the hands of all intelligent men and women who have received an education sufficient to enable them to read intelligently about such subjects as are discussed herein, and the number of such persons is very much larger than some people think."—*Congregationalist.*

"We have before had occasion to notice the force and elegance of this writer, and his new book shows scholarship even more advanced. * * * When we say, with some knowledge of how much is undertaken by the saying, that there is probably no book of moderate compass which combines in greater degree clearness of style with profundity of subject and of reasoning, we fulfil simple duty to an author whose success is all the more marked and gratifying from the multitude of kindred attempts with which we have been flooded from all sorts of pens."—*Presbyterian.*

"The book impresses us as clear, cogent and helpful, as vigorous in style as it is honest in purpose, and calculated to render valuable service in showing that religion and science are not antagonists but allies, and that both lead up toward the one God. We fancy that a good many readers of this volume will entertain toward the author a feeling of sincere personal gratitude."—*Boston Journal.*

"On the whole, we do not know of a book which may better be commended to thoughtful persons whose minds have been unsettled by objections of modern thought. It will be found a wholesome work for every minister in the land to read."
    —*Examiner and Chronicle.*

"It is a long time since we have met with an abler or fresher theological treatise than *Old Faiths in New Light*, by Newman Smyth, an author who in his work on "The Religious Feeling" has already shown ability as an expounder of Christian doctrine."—*Independent.*

*** *For sale by all booksellers, or sent postpaid, upon receipt of price,*
by

CHARLES SCRIBNER'S SONS,

NOS. 743 AND 745 BROADWAY, NEW YORK

THE
RELIGIOUS FEELING.

BY

Rev. NEWMAN SMYTH.

One Volume, 12mo, cloth, - - - - - - **$1.25.**

In this volume Mr. Smyth has it for his object to formulate the religious feeling as a capacity of the human mind, and to vindicate its claims to authority. He sets before himself at the outset the task of convicting sceptical philosophy out of its own mouth. The work is thoroughly logical, and displays a familiarity with the most recent German thought which is rarely to be found.

CRITICAL NOTICES.

MR. JOSEPH COOK'S opinion of " *The Religious Feeling:* "
" A fresh, keen book, copies of which I wish were scattered broadcast throughout the land : " and, in a letter to the author, " I admire exceedingly the familiarity you exhibit with the latest scientific literature. The reverent spirit with which you treat all Christian truth, the elegance of your style ; the searching originality of many a page in your volume, insure it a lasting, and, I hope, a wide usefulness."

" The argument in its clearness, force and illustrations, has never, to our knowledge, been better stated. Mr. Smyth has brought to his work a clear, analytical mind, an extensive knowledge of German philosophical thought, and an intellectual familiarity with the later English schools. He does his own thinking, and writes with perspicuity and vigor."—*The Advance.*

" Upon his own field of metaphysical and moral philosophy he displays a degree of clear, acute, and analytic reasoning which is of a high order and exceedingly effective, both in demolishing the semi-materialistic philosophy of Darwin and Spencer, and in demonstrating the spiritual nature and supernatural origin of the human soul."
—*Chicago Interior.*

" We welcome this volume as a valuable contribution to that type of thought in the vindication of theism which is specially demanded at the present time. The discussion throughout evinces much reading and vigorous thought, and is conducted with marked candor and ability."—*New Englander.*

" We can cordially recommend the reader to follow the author through his entire argument, for it is both brief and clear. The book will form a help to many perplexed minds, and it epitomizes very satisfactorily some of the best results of conservative German thought."—*Cincinnati Gazette.*

" This very interesting book is always eloquent and suggestive. What makes it especially noteworthy, seems to us its significance in relation to our day."
—*New York World.*

" The argument contained in these pages is eminently satisfactory. It is one of the best answers to Darwin and his followers we have ever met with."—*The Churchman.*

*** *For sale by all booksellers, or will be sent, prepaid, upon receipt of price,* by.

CHARLES SCRIBNER'S SONS,

NOS. 743 AND 745 BROADWAY, NEW YORK.

www.ingramcontent.com/pod-product-compliance
Lightning Source LLC
Chambersburg PA
CBHW031106020726
47495CB00007B/2075